Practical Research Methods for Media and Cultural Studies

Practical Research Methods for Media and Cultural Studies

Making People Count

Máire Messenger Davies and Nick Mosdell

Edinburgh University Press

© Máire Messenger Davies and Nick Mosdell, 2006

Edinburgh University Press Ltd
22 George Square, Edinburgh

Typeset in 11/13pt Monotype Baskerville by
Servis Filmsetting Ltd, Manchester, and
printed and bound in Great Britain by
MPG Books Ltd, Bodmin, Cornwall

A CIP record for this book is available from the British Library

ISBN-10 0 7486 2184 9 (hardback)
ISBN-13 978 0 7486 2184 2 (hardback)
ISBN-10 0 7486 2185 7 (paperback)
ISBN-13 978 0 7486 2185 9 (paperback)

The right of Máire Messenger Davies and Nick Mosdell
to be identified as authors of this work
has been asserted in accordance with
the Copyright, Designs and Patents Act 1988.

Contents

Acknowledgements

We would like to thank the following people for their contributions to this book: Sarah Edwards, Dr Claire Wardle and Dr Ema Sofia Leitao.

Everyone involved with the 'Consenting Children?' project – the staff at the BSC, the research team, and the children and families who participated.

Everyone involved with the West Yorkshire Playhouse project, especially Professor Roberta Pearson. Special thanks are due to Patrick Stewart for help with access.

All the students who have kindly allowed us to use examples of their work.

Finally, this book is dedicated to all the students, past, present and future, who have motivated us to develop our teaching courses and materials and who, unlikely though it may sound, have made the experience of teaching quantitative research methods rewarding and fun.

PART ONE

DESIGN: 'PLANNING IT'

CHAPTER 1

Introduction

> 'I am happy to teach them about research with
> people and audiences, but I can't do numbers.'

This remark, from a professor in Media Studies who had received a number of grants from the British Economic and Social Research Council to conduct research on questions of media representation, is typical of many scholars and students in the Humanities. You could throw a book in any number of Humanities departments in well-regarded universities and the chances of hitting somebody who 'can't do numbers' would be extremely high.

This book is for people who think they can't do numbers and moreover don't want to do them, perhaps because 'doing numbers', in the form of studying mathematics at school, has been associated with feelings of struggle, bewilderment and incompetence. For many such people, even if numbers eventually were mastered, numerical formulae still seem less adequate at explaining the complexity of the world, or of personal experiences, than language or artistic forms. This sense of inadequacy and boredom with numbers can be uncomfortable for bright, imaginative young people, used to succeeding intellectually in other areas of the curriculum based on linguistic and creative skills, such as English, history and the arts. Such feelings can lead to rejection and suspicion of any kind of knowledge which is based on the systematic acquisition of data analysed in numerical form; we have found this to be the case with many students and colleagues throughout our careers. Yet much of the everyday knowledge we all have about the world does come in numerical form, or can be translated into that form for easier manipulation and prediction. Often we do not realise that when we 'calculate the odds', we are dealing in mathematical probabilities, or that when we make value judgements about what is 'best', 'better' or 'worse', we are manipulating 'ordinal data'.

One example of a very common way in which we organise our knowledge about the world is through graded preferences or 'rankings' – an example drawn from popular culture is 'Top Tens'. Every student is familiar with such phenomena. 'Top Tens' can be based on your personal likes and dislikes, which may vary over time: your top ten favourite albums or movies today may be different this time next year. But they are still ranked from 1 (the best) to 10 (the 10th best – or worst), with 5 being in the middle (or is it? . . .). Rankings may also be based on more systematic and large-scale number-crunching, as with the commercial industry Top Tens, which are derived from the number of sales of a recording, or, in the case of movies, from the number of people paying to go to see a film in the first weekend of its release. These numbers are *precisely measurable* and are based on *accurate counting* at sales points of the numbers of tickets sold.

Unlike your personal tastes, this way of counting *won't* vary (as such, it is called 'interval data'), but the figures amassed in this way can affect your personal preferences just the same. Collecting precise records of what kind of product does well at the box office will affect what becomes available to you as a cultural consumer next year. If the current fashion in cinema production is for fantasy (*Harry Potter, Lord of the Rings*), the chances of next year's cinematic offerings including fantasy films are going to be greater. These 'chances' are not in fact 'chance' (we'll say more about 'chance' in Chapter 10); the odds of repeating the success of a *Harry Potter* will be very precisely calculated by the financial and marketing advisers to the Hollywood production companies.

Getting a degree and getting a job

If you are a Humanities student, it is likely that at some stage you will be required to study a research methods module or course. This is particularly the case for postgraduate students, and increasingly so for undergraduates. We have found that some colleagues in Humanities departments are a bit sceptical about 'methodology' and the possibility of teaching 'how to do research'. Research is just something you do. We have found that our practical approach to teaching quantitative methods – which can also be applied to other methods – has helped to bridge this perceptual gap. This book is a basic introduction to the principles of empirical quantitative research, many of which, we believe, underpin *any* effective approach to methodology teaching. These principles state that research should be rigorous, systematic, replicable, valid, derived from clear research questions and properly operationalised, whatever your subject area. The book describes pedagogic procedures which, in our experience, have been effective with students who are highly resistant to the idea of 'statistics', 'scientific methods' or 'measuring' abstract concepts.

As a Humanities student it is also likely that you will be seeking employment in the cultural or service (whether public or private) industries when you graduate. If you want to work in the cultural industries at any level – whether in production, or administration or management, or marketing, or training, or government policy (as in the Department of Culture, Media and Sport in Britain, or the Federal Communications Commission in the United States) – you will need to understand something about the kinds of calculations made from box office and sales figures and – more controversially – the assumptions about audiences and their feelings, which are sometimes inferred from these calculations. You will need to understand how to interpret figures and how to be sceptical of some of the claims you will hear based on them. The best way to understand a procedure, we believe, is to learn to *do it yourself*. Hence this book.

This book is primarily a practical guide to the uses of quantitative (numerical) research methods in the Humanities, with particular reference to different kinds of media and cultural research. Before we get down to the specific details of designing and carrying out such a research project, we want to say something about the historical and intellectual background to the systematic study of human beings and their tastes, feelings, attitudes and behaviour – the disciplines of social science, from which quantitative research methods are mainly drawn.

'How can you study human beings as if they were specimens?' The case for social science

A common difficulty for Humanities students in studying social science research methods is the word 'science'. As with mathematics, science may be associated with difficulty and failure at school; also with dehumanising formulae, experiments, laboratories, abstractions, 'men in white coats', and various moral, social and political ills – nuclear weapons, environmental degradation, cruelty to animals, 'playing God' by cloning embryos, colonial exploitation of developing countries, and so on. Many of people's notions about science come from popular media: from dystopic movies of the future in which current problems brought about by human scientific and technological overkill create terrifying threats to humanity: *Blade Runner*; *Soylent Green*; *Logan's Run*; *The Day after Tomorrow*, and so on. The fact that science provides major solutions in helping to solve these problems may sometimes be forgotten because such solutions are cumulative and incremental, and have much less narrative and spectacular potential as stories.

Conversely, the human impact of scientific development may sometimes be overlooked by 'pure' scientists (those who study the 'natural' sciences such as physics, chemistry, biology). Fantasy stories express these human anxieties in ways that scientists and policy-makers would do well to address. Also, science can only work well within human social institutions which are rationally and compassionately organised and which allow scope for human imagination, creativity and instincts for ethical behaviour. A laboratory is a human social institution too, and as such can be studied using **social scientific methods**.

What are workable social systems? The uses of social science

Social science raises, and helps to answer, questions that the natural sciences tend to take as given and that people in the Humanities may argue can be answered purely by critical analysis and interpretation: the question of how we bring about workable social arrangements in which both science and the arts can flourish in the first place. How do we understand the human organisations, whether family groups, schools, nation-states or workplaces, that appear to work effectively, and how can we learn and apply lessons from them in order to ensure that new social arrangements will also work well? Similarly, where human social organisations do not appear to be working well – where there is conflict, relationship breakdown, extreme poverty, inequality, abuse or crime – how do we understand these phenomena, and how can we put them right?

In the field of media, culture and communications – the study of the myriad ways in which human beings acquire and convey meaning about themselves and to others – social science may seem even less relevant. In fact, it can raise, and help to answer, many useful questions:

- How does language develop in the first place, and how can we devise reliable methods of evaluating the way that babies communicate, given that they don't yet use words?[1]
- What forms of communication do different kinds of people use, and how might this differently affect their perceptions of meanings?
- What difference do culture, ethnicity and genetic inheritance make to people's communication behaviours, creativity and tastes?
- What factors determine the industrial production and distribution of commercial media products?
- What is the degree of public support for public service media?
- How do media institutions change over time?
- What is the relationship between art, culture, media and government?
- How do you evaluate, compare and predict different people's tastes, comprehension, influence or susceptibility to persuasion?
- What makes people change their attitudes?
- What makes people want to buy things? Or not buy them?
- How do different people set a value on media products – whether economic, political, cultural or moral?
- How do people *learn* to make sense of different forms of communication? How do they adapt to 'new' media?
- Where do 'new' media come from?
- Do we learn more from images or from words?
- What stops people understanding and learning effectively?
- How do we distinguish between propaganda and 'truth'?
- When people have learned something, what makes them forget it again?
- Does watching violent films make children violent?
- What is violence anyway?

---

[1] M. M. Davies, E. Lloyd and A. Scheffler (1987) *Baby Language*, London: Unwin Hyman.

And so on, and on.

These are questions which the social sciences: psychology, socio-logy, anthropology – the study of human beings and their behaviour – can help to answer. Indeed, they are the kinds of questions that are much more likely to be *asked* by social scientists than by other scholars. An art critic may value and write about 'creativity' or 'originality' in a work of art. The social scientist asks:

> 'What does the term creativity *mean* to the people who use it? Who does use it? And how might they apply it in their everyday lives and jobs?'

Scientific method

A major usefulness of science as applied to the study of human beings, we want to argue, is its *method*. There are many ways of study-ing human beings, but the quantitative research methods we write about in this book are based on rigorous and systematic procedures drawn from science, and these research design procedures are very useful tools, not only for research, but for logical thinking generally. Learning these procedures provides 'transferable skills' which can be used in all walks of life. This book is a simple introduction to such methodologies. It does not pretend to be a guide to carrying out complex professional research projects, such as social policy surveys or criminological or educational experiments. It is a guide for the classroom; a way of learning (and teaching) social scientific proce-dures, specifically quantitative research methods, which can be prac-tically and (we hope) relatively painlessly applied within an academic teaching programme. This could be:

- a research methods course for postgraduate training; or
- an undergraduate research methods dissertation module; or
- a short, intensive research methods workshop for professional short courses; or
- a short workshop within a larger research methods training pro-gramme, like those we have conducted at Cardiff University.

As such, this book may seem to some fully-fledged social scientists, whether in universities or outside them, shockingly simple and basic, and sadly lacking in the more sophisticated, complex, mathematical research techniques employed, for instance, in advanced experimental psychology or in major social policy surveys. As former psychology postgraduates and researchers, we have done a bit of advanced experimental psychology ourselves; we have even helped out on some social policy surveys and know what the possibilities are for answering complex questions in these research areas, especially with the exciting new software packages for designing and conducting statistical and other kinds of research which have been produced since we began our own studies. All we can say in defence of our simplistic approach is that most of the many students to whom we have taught research methods over the years don't want to be experimental psychologists or social policy researchers: they want to be film-makers, or journalists, or PR executives, or teachers, or just want to get a good degree and go travelling. But they do need to carry out research as part of their educational training, and – heretical thought – they do have some expectations that carrying out a practical project, including doing research with numbers, ought to be enjoyable and enlightening, even fun. We think so too.

Introducing social science research on the media: background reading

This is primarily a 'how to' book, but it is also important for students to understand some of the intellectual background of the social sciences as well as some of the history of empirical research into the media. Therefore, we recommend some basic reading before embarking on detailed methods training. Every teacher and student may have their pet textbooks or theorists who are useful to them, but two key texts in media research which we have found valuable and which flesh out in more detail some of the procedures we talk about in this book are Wimmer and Dominick's *Mass Media Research*, now in its eighth edition (2006), and Bauer and Gaskell's edited collection, *Qualitative Research with Image Text and Sound* (2000). Williams' *Science and Social Science: An Introduction* (London and New York: Routledge, 2000) is also a useful account of the conceptual and methodological commonalities and distinctions between pure science and its application to human activities. Williams makes a helpful distinction between scientific method and the social constructionism and relativism of cultural studies:

> An important task of science and one in which it is (I think) partially successful, is to distinguish between the 'real' and what is socially constructed as 'real' . . . gravity for example does not differentially affect cultures in time or space. (p. 85)

It is also useful for students to be aware of general theoretical debates surrounding the operation of human institutions such as the media, and their political, economic and social roles, as well as their historical origins. Jürgen Habermas's work on 'the public sphere' underpins much of the thinking about the social role of media institutions and he has articulated the value of empirical evidence and systematic and rigorous ways of gathering it:

> we consider methods and procedures of gathering and presenting evidence as essential for social scientific research . . . they place research squarely within the public sphere and subject it to the demands of accountability. Methods and procedures are the scientific way of being publicly accountable for evidence. However, we have to assume a public sphere that is free to allow the uncensored pursuit of evidence, which is not to be taken for granted. (Habermas, 1989; quoted in Bauer and Gaskell 2000, p. 12)

The claim here is that social scientific methods make research publicly 'accountable' – that is, they provide a guarantee of a minimum level of reliability, consistency, validity and replicability because these are universally accepted procedures which are in the public domain and can be used and checked by other scholars and by other people generally; this is necessary in a democracy. Habermas makes a warning point that 'the uncensored pursuit of evidence' is 'not to be taken for granted'. Under some forms of government 'uncensored pursuit of evidence' could be seen as a challenge to the ruling powers. Although learning how to design a standardised questionnaire and to analyse the results using proven statistical techniques may not seem like a particularly heroic enterprise in the advancement of human enlightenment, there is a sense in which it does have this heroic aspect: these methods are an attempt to make knowledge independent, and not reliant on human subjectivity, 'instinct', emotional reactions, common sense, mere habit or authority. There is a long history of totalitarian regimes threatening scientific enquiry; young people who challenge received wisdom – who ask 'why?' or 'how?' or 'why not?' – may get into trouble if they live in communities where challenging traditional modes of thought is discouraged.

Scientific method not only does not *dis*courage challenges to received wisdom; it positively *en*courages them.

The scientific method

Scientific method – the empirical testing of hypotheses – can be distinguished from other sources of knowledge, such as:

a) **Tenacity**, or tradition: 'We've always done it this way. What's good enough for the people who came before us is good enough for us.'
b) **Intuition**: the 'gut feeling' that can't be put into words, which many creative people talk about when asked why or how they did something.
c) **Authority**: religious texts; parents; famous authors: 'I believe it because a particular authority, or guru, says so.'

In contrast, the scientific community and the discoveries produced within it have different characteristics: scientific knowledge is often **anonymous**. Although discoveries may be associated with particular individuals, the process of acquiring scientific information depends on many people and teams working over time. Hence scientific knowledge is **cumulative** and **reactive** (research is done in response to other people's research). It is a kind of jigsaw in which no one individual can be dominant – unlike in the arts, where (despite French theorists announcing 'the death of the author') the study of individual artists and authors historically, economically and critically, is still central to scholarship.

Scientific characteristics

Science is:

1. **Public**: known and available for testing and especially for *replication* (see Chapters 2 and 3).
2. **Objective**: scientific method attempts to rule out, or control for, subjective judgements; for example, behaviour is seen as a more

reliable indicator of someone's state of mind than an observer's interpretation. If you want to demonstrate that someone's attention is not held by a TV programme, seeing them switching the TV off is a more reliable measure (because directly observable and not subject to interpretation) than trying to analyse the facial expression of the viewer.

3. **Empirical**: knowable, measurable, based on evidence. Abstract concepts, such as 'boredom', as above, have to be *operationally defined* (see Chapter 2).

4. **Systematic and cumulative**, based on methods which can be known and shared by all scholars everywhere, and hence built on, adapted, revised, extended, changed by other scholars.

Quality versus quantity?

In their book about qualitative research (that is, research which is not based on numerical analysis or scientific procedures such as experiments, but is based on individual observation and critical analysis), Bauer and Gaskell argue that such research can learn a lot from scientific methods. Among the advantages they claim for science are:

- procedural clarity – a set of steps and activities which are generally universally agreed on by quantitative researchers;
- 'a developed discourse on quality in the research process which establishes a basis for self-criticism'. Such an emphasis on quality in the research process:
- serves to demarcate good from bad practice,
- helps to establish credibility in the context of publicly accountable research, and, as we have argued,
- these procedures are a valuable didactic tool in the training of students.

The purpose of science is to make valid predictions, based on 'empirically supported universal laws', which, under certain conditions (which may vary), can be predicted with some certainty to operate in the same way more than once.

Bauer and Gaskell also scrutinise what they call the 'stronger claim often made for qualitative research that it is intrinsically a more critical and potentially emancipatory form of research' (2000, p. 14). Qualitative research aims to see through the eyes of those being studied. It is seen as necessary to understand the interpretations that social actors (people themselves) have of the world, because it is these interpretations that motivate the behaviour that creates the social world itself. However, as these authors point out, it does not necessarily follow that the outcome is a critical piece of work. Understanding may also 'serve as a basis for the establishment of mechanisms of social control'. Quantitative and qualitative methodologies need to be compared in terms not only of how reliable and replicable they are, but also how sensitive they are to the needs, rights and points of view of the people, or groups, being studied. Both kinds of method need techniques which respect these needs and rights and do not assert or privilege the personal points of view of the people doing the research.

Falsifying hypotheses

One further important characteristic of scientific method is that it is often 'counter-intuitive' – that is, it seems to fly in the face of common sense. One of the most difficult things for beginners in research methodology to grasp is the notion of falsification (more is said about this and about the 'null hypothesis' in Chapter 2). As we've said, science – no matter how objective, rigorous and replicable its procedures may be – still operates within fallible human institutions, and one of the most enlightening books on how science itself changes historically and culturally is Thomas Kuhn's *The Structure of Scientific Revolutions* (1970). Kuhn states:

> Few philosophers of science still seek absolute criteria for the verification of scientific theories. Noting that no theory can ever be exposed to all possible relevant tests, they ask not whether a theory has been verified but rather about its probability in the light of the evidence that actually exists. (p. 145)

Kuhn refers to the work of the philosopher Karl Popper,[2] who, says Kuhn, 'denies the existence of any verification procedures at all'. Popper emphasises the importance of 'falsification': a test that,

---

[2] K. R. Popper (1959) *The Logic of Scientific Discovery*, New York: Basic Books.

'because its outcome is negative, necessitates the rejection of an established theory'. This approach – that you can't prove anything, you can only disprove it – may sound somewhat negative to the beginning researcher. It is also counter-intuitive. By trying to falsify your hypotheses rather than to support them, it would seem that all you're doing with your research is knocking down ideas, rather than building them up. Where can new knowledge come from in this case?

In fact, 'falsification' is not only important intellectually, it is also a practical way of keeping your project manageable, especially important for amateur and student researchers with limited resources. As Kuhn says, 'no theory can ever be exposed to all possible relevant tests', not even by full-time professional scientists or social scientists, never mind a student on a one-year MA course. A useful way of showing how sensible 'falsification' is as a way of limiting and making research design manageable comes from Jean Aitchison in her book on language, *The Articulate Mammal* (1983):

> The point is, science proceeds by *disproving* hypotheses. Suppose you were interested in flowers. You might formulate a hypothesis, 'All roses are white, red, pink, orange or yellow.' There would be absolutely no point at all in collecting hundreds, thousands, or even millions of white, red, pink, orange and yellow roses. You would merely be collecting additional evidence consistent with your hypothesis. If you were genuinely interested in making a botanical advance, you would send people in all directions hunting for black, blue, mauve or green roses. Your hypothesis would stand until somebody found a blue rose. Then in theory you should be delighted that botany had made progress and found out about blue roses. Naturally when you formulate a hypothesis it has to be one which is capable of disproof. A hypothesis such as 'Henry VIII would have disliked spaceships' cannot be disproved and consequently is useless. (pp. 187–8)

The social scientific study of the media

Social science methods began to be applied to the media as the result of a number of political and historical developments. During the twentieth century, particularly arising from the First World War, and even more during and after the Second World War, a concern with propaganda and its effects led to the academic study of mass media institutions and politics, particularly broadcast media – first radio, then television. This was also linked with the development of behaviourist psychology in the 1930s and 1940s, leading to what has been popularly called 'the magic bullet', or 'hypodermic needle', theory of media effects: the view that people will be influenced directly by examples of behaviour they see in film and television, and will therefore imitate them. Further developments leading to systematic research into the relationship of the media with society included the growth of advertising and the consumer society, particularly in the United States. There was also public concern especially about children and other vulnerable groups in their susceptibility to harmful media effects.[3]

As media institutions became more powerful economically and politically, with increased competition for advertising income and hence for the attention of the public, the question of how to attract and mould public attitudes became more pressing for media institutions themselves. The television ratings (audience measurement) are a major example of how systematic audience research, based on large-scale quantitative surveys, is absolutely central to the operation and economic survival of broadcasting. Within educational establishments, and also within many media and cultural institutions, other kinds of questions about how effective particular creative techniques could be in helping people learn and understand also stimulated research. An example is the formative and evaluative research for the preschool programme *Sesame Street* (see Lesser, 1974),[4] which continues to this day, and guides production decisions.

This book and what it will do

So, this book can be summarised as a 'Rough Guide' to social science research methods, aimed at empowering Humanities students and helping them in a sympathetic way to master complex research skills. It aims to show how different disciplinary research approaches can be integrated. It particularly demonstrates how quantitative research

---

[3] See e.g. A. Bandura et al. (1963) 'Imitation of film-mediated aggressive models', *Journal of Abnormal and Social Psychology*, vol.66, No.1, 3–11, and the many similar experiments 'replicating' his findings

[4] G. Lesser (1974) *Children and Television: Lessons from Sesame Street*, New York: Random House.

methods, including statistical surveys and content analysis, can be used to answer qualitative questions about, for instance, audience tastes, interpretation of texts and the relationship of demographic factors, such as social class and gender, to cultural consumption and behaviour. All of this is illustrated with examples drawn from our teaching and student work.

The book aims particularly to show how students' *own* choices of 'themes, concepts and ideas' can be refined to produce manageable research questions, and how – depending on the choice of theme – an appropriate research method and design can be formulated. The book will focus on quantitative approaches, such as surveys and content analysis; however, qualitative approaches, such as focus groups, discourse analysis and case studies, although technically 'left out', will be touched on, since multiple methods – or 'triangulation' – are necessary for humanities-type research questions. We will leave out dense theoretical discussions, since the book is meant to be a practical and accessible work of reference and advice. There will also be no complicated mathematical formulae. We will base our explanations on the standard SPSS tabulated printouts, as we do in class, with our own 'glosses' written in clear language to help students understand what they are doing.

What will readers gain from it?

Readers will gain:

a) mastery of something they may have found difficult and inaccessible, and therefore a real sense of achievement;
b) mastery of computer technology, and familiarity with a powerful and complex analytical computer program;
c) transferable intellectual skills, such as a critical approach to numbers and statistical claims; an ability to interpret research reports and surveys; problem-solving; precise formulation of research questions, methods and goals;
d) real-world applications of research skills, based on students' own ideas and interests;
e) for teachers, useful tools and teaching approaches – as well as knowledge and skills for themselves.

CHAPTER 2

What is Your Research Question?

This chapter deals with one of the most difficult issues for students, and it comes right at the start of the project, which can lead to a feeling of 'why bother?' This is the task of formulating a precise research question. How, for instance, can a feeling that:

> **'the press is biased'**, or that
> **'advertising exploits women'**, or that
> **'children are corrupted by violence on television'**

– topics proposed by many students for their dissertation projects, reflecting popularly held beliefs – be translated into a practicable research question and project?

Students often choose a dissertation or research project topic because they have a strong 'gut feeling' about a particular issue – and this can be a good way to start. It's very hard to investigate something for several months (or for PhD students, years) when you have no particular emotional investment in it. However, emotional investment can be a drawback, because it creates – yes – 'bias'. Many students are convinced that something is already the case ('I know that advertising really does exploit women'). But why bother to carry out research, if you already know the answer? The first step in the art of producing a good and do-able research topic for a student project or dissertation consists in coming up with a question *which needs an answer*, in other words, which requires some research. Second, it has to be a practicable question which can be answered during the time-scale and the research resources of the course you are studying.

In this chapter we will address the following key preliminary issues in choosing and setting up a design for a research project:

- practicability;
- formulating the question;
- formulating a hypothesis;
- the concept of the 'null hypothesis';
- validity;

- generalisability;
- the 'wh' questions: what, why, where, when, how and with whom?
- Group versus individual projects

Practicability

It is essential to point out from the beginning that student projects are limited in terms of what they can do: limited in time, in financial resources and in access to specialised research resources such as visits to overseas archives or to eminent interviewees. A good student project should thus not be too ambitious in its scope. If you are writing a master's or undergraduate dissertation, it is likely that you will have at the most six months in which to carry out the project and write it up. Even if you are a PhD student with three years to complete your project, your time needs to be carefully managed: good forward design and planning are essential if you are intending to carry out empirical work, particularly fieldwork with human subjects. Fieldwork will always require a *pilot study* (see Chapter 8), and this increases the amount of time needed to collect and analyse data.

It is wise for people teaching dissertation modules to ensure that students' topics are chosen and their methods decided on fairly early in the academic year during which the project must be carried out (see Chapter 12 for more advice for teachers on this). As mentioned, planning, piloting, carrying out and analysing fieldwork takes time and you are unlikely to have large amounts of external research funding for a student project. Hence, if you wish to study the alleged bias in the press in your own country (assuming you are an international student from, say, Africa, Asia or Europe, as many of our students are), it is not practicable to finance a special trip to do this. However, with the kind of good forward planning we are recommending in this book, it may be possible to combine a holiday visit home with fieldwork or archive work. Many of our students have done this.

Formulating the question

The key issue is: *what do you want to know?*

Let us take the question of 'bias in the press', using a real example from the country in which one of us is working, Northern Ireland. An MA student in an introductory research class said he was interested in studying 'press coverage of the North'.

How might we refine this topic and turn it into a practicable research question and project? For a start we need to define terms – we need to provide what are called '**operational definitions**' of this topic.

First, 'the North'. Does he mean Northern Ireland or the North of some other place? He means Northern Ireland, and the use of the term 'North' immediately implies the existence of an alternative – 'South'. In the case of Ireland, the term 'South' connotes both a political and a geographic entity: the 'opposite' of Northern Ireland is the Republic of Ireland, often called 'the South of Ireland', even though the most northerly county of the island of Ireland, Donegal, is in the Republic, whereas Northern Ireland is part of the United Kingdom. Hence, our student's research question has a number of hidden complexities; he might want to include an element of contrast between 'North' and 'South' and between the two different political situations in the two parts of Ireland. This student is studying journalism and it turns out he is interested in the political situation in Northern Ireland. So his topic is not 'the North' in general, but needs to be redefined as 'politics in Northern Ireland'.

Next 'the press': Does this mean newspapers? Printed or online? British newspapers? Irish newspapers? International newspapers? Local or national newspapers? *All* newspapers from the time they were first printed or just some of them, and if only some of them, on what basis would his selection (or **sample** – see more about this in Chapter 4) be made? This student did mean newspapers, but was not sure at this stage if he wanted to look at both British and Irish newspapers, or why this might be a relevant decision to his project, since he did not yet know what his research question was in any detail. Hence the importance of deciding precisely what the research question will be: only then can appropriate decisions be taken about **method**.

Finally 'coverage': does this mean the sheer *amount* of 'coverage' – the number of stories, or column inches, devoted to the North of Ireland – or does it mean the way in which these stories are written and presented (something more intangible and difficult to define)? (We will come to this in our chapter on **content analysis**; see Chapter 7.) Again, the answer to this will vary depending on the precise research question.

Given that it transpires that this student is worried about possible 'bias' in the reporting of Northern Irish politics, before we go any further, it is important to find an **operational definition** of what he means by bias. Bias towards? Bias against? Bias on the part of individual reporters? Or bias on the part of the editorial line of the paper generally?

What does bias look like?

Answering questions like this is one of the hardest things for Humanities students to do: to produce an **operational definition** of an abstract concept. Those of us trained in the social sciences – in our case, psychology – had to learn how to do this, sometimes with difficulty, in setting up experiments to measure human reactions and emotions. For instance, one measure of bias in a psychology experiment could be *reaction time* in carrying out a task: if asked to press a button to say whether they agreed or disagreed that a particular Irish politician was 'trustworthy', a person biased in favour of the politician would find it easier to press the button marked 'agree' and is likely to react more quickly than someone who disagreed. (Negative judgements take longer to process mentally.)

The operational definition of bias here is thus:

'*Speed of reaction to a statement about the politician's character.*'

Another operational definition of bias – this time in the case of written text – could be:

The use of negative language in reporting.

Bias in press coverage could be recognised by the consistent use of negative terms about a politician, such as 'ANGER AT' or 'LACK OF TRUST CLAIM' in headlines about him. You will note that terms like these include a further operational definition of possible bias in that they are:

reported reactions, not actual factual evidence

of the man's untrustworthiness.

Formulating a hypothesis

Question or hypothesis? Do it both ways

So is our student any nearer to formulating a research question? Before we come up with some possible questions arising out of the preliminary refining and defining processes described above, we need to alert the novice researcher to one more important approach: the need to have a **hypothesis**. A hypothesis is an assumption, or hunch, that something is likely to be the case; your research will test whether your assumption is right or not. For instance, in the case of bias in the press, your hypothesis, or hunch, might be that 'the press is biased against Northern Irish politicians'. In such a case, we can see that the *method* question about which particular newspapers we are going to study is very important. We might expect that newspapers published in England (such as the national dailies, originating in London) are more likely to be biased against Northern Irish politicians than Irish newspapers, whether in the North or South. This bias might express itself in sheer lack of coverage (as measured by number of stories, or column inches) in English newspapers, compared with Irish newspapers. Or our researcher might want to compare newspapers in the Republic of Ireland with newspapers in the North of Ireland in terms of the emotive language they use. Or he might want to compare newspapers in the North only, and look at publications with differing political constituencies among their readers and study how they report on the 'others'. *It all depends on what the research question is.* Thus, we see that no decisions about research methods (which newspapers, how many, where we should look for them, how we analyse them) can be taken until the research question/hypothesis is properly formulated.

Preliminary research question about press bias and Northern Irish politics

We do have the beginnings of a research question which can also be expressed as a hypothesis. It may well be that this question will be further refined once the student embarks on the research, but it is better to be clear from the outset what you want to know before you get going on time-consuming and possibly expensive data-gathering. Phrased as a question, the student's inquiry could be:

> To what extent do newspapers originating in England differ from newspapers published in Northern Ireland in a) the amount and b) the emotional tone of their coverage of Northern Irish politicians?

Preliminary hypothesis based on this question
This can also be expressed as a hypothesis:

> It is predicted that newspapers originating in England will be a) less likely to give lengthy coverage and b) more likely to give negative coverage of Northern Irish politicians than newspapers originating in Northern Ireland.

You can see that turning the question into a hypothesis gives the researcher something to go on. You have a working assumption to guide your search for evidence and your analysis. Of course your hypothesis may be wrong – it may turn out that you cannot find evidence of this kind of bias in your study. But that is the purpose of research: to test hypotheses and – quite often – to show that, at least from the evidence you have gathered, these assumptions cannot be supported after all. (We will say more about the **null hypothesis** and other hypothesis-testing procedures later.) The purpose of empirical research is never to reinforce or prove what you think you know already; it is to put this knowledge to the test and to question how reliable it is by seeking evidence.

The source of hypotheses: reviewing the literature
The final point to emphasise in this early stage of formulating your topic is to stress the importance of acquiring solid background knowledge of the topic you are interested in through appropriate reading; a review of this reading material (**literature review**) will be the first chapter of a thesis. Our student who wanted to study the press coverage of Northern Irish politics had some preliminary knowledge of Irish politics, but before finally deciding on his research question, it will be important for him to read some existing studies, first, of media coverage of Northern Ireland (such as Bill Rolston and David Miller (eds.) (1996) *War and Words: The Northern Ireland Media Reader*), and second,

some more general studies to help with methodology: how to evaluate media 'bias' (for instance, the work of the Glasgow Media Group on television news coverage, or the major study of the British press by James Curran and Jean Seaton (1997) *Power without Responsibility*). From this background reading he will be able to develop a research question arising from these earlier studies, perhaps applying lessons learned by researchers in Glasgow to the Northern Irish situation.

The null hypothesis

Before we leave the topic of hypotheses, we must briefly mention another concept that can be quite difficult for many Humanities (and other) students to grasp: the concept of the 'null hypothesis'. The null hypothesis states that 'there is *no difference* between any particular sets of observations' – whether these observations suggest that the British press is more hostile to Irish politicians than the Irish press, or vice versa. The null hypothesis assumes that any observed differences are likely to be due to *chance*, not to 'bias' or to any other deliberate or intentional process. It is this assumption – that observed differences in your data are due only to chance – that is tested in statistical tests. We will say more about these tests later; at this stage all we will say is that it is likely that you, as a keen researcher, will be hoping that the null hypothesis will *not* be supported by your research; in other words, you hope that the evidence that you have collected about bias in the press (or whatever topic you are studying) is so repeated and systematic, that it must be due to deliberate intention, not to chance. You may be wrong though, and you must not allow your *own* desires and intentions to distort the research process. Hence the importance of proper design and method in research.

The null hypothesis is a technical way of expressing what we discussed in the introductory chapter – Popper's concept of the *falsification* of hypotheses. Assumptions must be challenged, not just supported, by the research process.

Validity

The next key term to take account of in designing a good empirical study is **validity**, or making your study *reliable*. It is important to note that in social science we do not use the term 'truth' about the findings of a study. We call our findings 'valid' – that is, they are as reliable as they can be at the present moment (but times and circumstances may change, which could lead to different findings being produced in a future study). Our findings are valid because we have made every effort to ensure that there were no avoidable mistakes in the way we designed and carried out the study. We also do not use the term 'prove' because absolute proof is impossible in an area of study – the social sciences – where human judgements, emotions and cultural variability are so diverse and complex.

We don't use the term 'true' because for every categorical statement you might make about human beings and their behaviour –

'men like fighting',
'women care a lot about what they look like',
'children are innocent'

– you can always find counter-examples: men who don't like fighting, women who don't care about fashion, children who appear to be evil incarnate. The most we can ever do is 'provide convincing evidence' that, given certain circumstances, and given the selected sample, in most of the examples we've gathered something appears to be the case; but we can never conclusively 'prove' it.

In seeking evidence, in order to make our study 'valid', we have to design our study so that mistakes don't creep into the findings. Because of human variability and human fallibility, there will always be some margin of error in any scientific or social scientific study. This 'error' value is factored into statistical tests looking at whether the results of a study are significant or not; all numerical analysis recognises that there will be some sources of error. Error can never be eliminated, only minimised and factored into the final statistical analysis.

Again, the importance of choosing a precise and specific research question helps to minimise error in the final analysis. For instance, in the case of Northern Ireland, it is much easier to demonstrate that some newspapers devote less *space* to Irish politics, or use more *negative language* in headlines, than it is to 'prove' that:

'Most English journalists are historically prejudiced against Ireland because the Brits can't be trusted when it comes to Ireland'

as some populist views might have it. Space and words are measurable; they can be counted (whether through column inches, or through the number of negative words as a proportion of all words) and, more importantly, they can be *checked by another researcher* to make sure that they have been counted accurately. (This is called '**intercoder reliability**'; we say more about it in Chapter 7.) If your unit of measurement has been chosen carefully (that is, if it is reliably measurable, as inches or emotive words are), then people who are able to count, regardless of their cultural or demographic background, will come up with the same answers as you do. With such an exercise, you may not prove much about the origins of supposed historical prejudices, but you may be able to demonstrate what you set out to do: that there is a persistent negative bias in two key attributes of the British press in its coverage of Ireland, these key attributes being space and language.

So, the most important thing we have to do in designing our research project to ensure validity is to minimise the chances of error.

There are two key aspects to validity: *external* and *internal*.

External validity

External validity has been defined by Wimmer and Dominick (1994, p. 35) as 'how well the results of a study can be generalized across populations, settings and time'. When a study is externally valid it means that we can apply its findings to other similar people, or similar texts, in similar situations, which didn't take part in our study. To make the study externally valid, the sample of people, or material, that we choose to study (and remember, as we said above, you can never study everything – you always have to make a selection) must be **representative** of the people or material you are interested in.

For instance, we can take an example from a student project carried out at Cardiff comparing the drinking habits of postgraduate and undergraduate students, including males and females. In this case, it was essential that whoever the researchers asked to take part in their project, these people a) needed to be students, b) should include roughly equal numbers of postgraduates and undergraduates, c) should include roughly equal numbers of males and females, and d) should include people who liked a drink sometimes. In other words, the sample had to be *representative* of the student drinker population of

Introduction - the effects of drinking

- Each of us drinks equivalent of 28 bottles of vodka a year

- 70% of hospital admissions at weekend are alcohol-related.

- Binge drinking causes rapid damage to the brain.

- Medical bill for binge drinking is £3 billion which is 12% of total amount NHS spends on its hospitals

Figure 2.1 From 'Binge Britain: Drinking Trends in University Students', Cardiff University MA research project by Sara Glynn, Miniushka Mujtaba, Andrea Doungas, Catherine Cunningham, Karl Tufuoh, 2005

Cardiff. The sample was of 100 students randomly chosen – that is, the researchers made no special effort to select particular kinds of people, they simply asked whoever walked by. But they made sure that their final 100 had the necessary equal proportions of postgrads, undergrads, males and females. (More will be said about random sampling and other forms of sampling in Chapter 4.)

In a real-life study, with more resources, the researchers would have wanted to have a bigger sample, including students from universities across the country, and students with different social, geographical or ethnic backgrounds. But for the purposes of a student research project, 100 students, fifty in each category, was a reasonably representative group to answer the questions about alcohol consumption that our researchers were interested in. By making sure their sample was reasonably representative of the group they were interested in, they ensured that their project had external validity.

Internal validity

Internal validity means making sure that your findings are as reliable as they can be because you have eliminated all possible sources of error in the way you have designed your study. Problems of design that could invalidate your study's findings include the following.

1. Problems with subjects

People change over time; in the case of a long-term (*longitudinal*) study, people change in ways that are nothing to do with what's happening in the project and that could affect their responses to your questions. In the case of a long-term study of bias among journalists on a newspaper with a particular political agenda, the staff on the paper might change their jobs, or the journalists in question might change their views, or simply get better at their job. Their opinions can't just be attributed to the paper's editorial line, or the diktats of its proprietor, or whatever you think the reasons for 'bias' might be.

In the case of children in particular, *maturation* is a factor – children grow up and change very quickly, and the younger they are, the more rapid and profound are these changes. There are solutions to these problems, the most common being a '*control group*' of people who are similar to the people in your study, but not taking part in it. Let us say, in a study of primary school children, that they were being observed to evaluate their responses to an educational TV programme over the period of a broadcast season: six months. The researchers might be interested in children's understanding of gender roles and the programme could be showing non-stereotypical activities for boys and girls. Your control group would be a similar group of children who were *not* being shown this educational programme. Each group would be evaluated on its attitude to gender roles at the beginning and at the end of the six months. Changes might come about in both groups as a result of maturation. But the research expectation would be that that those who saw the non-stereotypical gender programme would have changed *more* in their attitudes towards gender than those who did not see the programme.

2. Demand characteristics

The other main problem threatening internal validity is 'demand characteristics' – the problem we've already mentioned of your bias and your perhaps unconscious desire to point the people in your study towards particular answers or particular responses. There are ways round this too, including using people who do not have a stake in the study as interviewers, or using the more anonymous technique of the questionnaire. We say more about this extremely valuable research tool in later chapters.

Other problems that can lead to invalid results include problems with equipment such as faulty computer programs or out-of-date test procedures, and a phenomenon known as *statistical regression*. This means that in any accumulation of statistical information, there will be a 'regression towards the mean', a numerical drift towards the average score, which is a mathematical artefact. In layperson's language, 'things even out by themselves', not because of anything anybody has consciously done.

3. The risk of only doing it once: replication

Ideally, all studies should first be *piloted* to iron out snags of procedure, such as not having reliable computer programs or not having comprehensible questions in your questionnaire. Students can certainly manage to carry out pilots; even just trying out your research instrument (your questionnaire, your interview schedule or content coding sheet) on a few friends enables you to make useful practical decisions, such as whether your procedures take too long, or whether the questions you ask make sense to people whose first language isn't English. But even more ideal is to carry out the main study more than once – to *replicate* it. If, using the same procedures and similar groups of people (or similar material in the case of content analysis), you get broadly the same results each time, then you have a reliable, solid, valid set of findings, which can be published and be useful to other scholars. It isn't usually possible for student projects to be replicated because of lack of time and resources, but sometimes, if you have done a good undergraduate project, you can do it again, in more depth and with more resources, at postgraduate level. This can be a form of replication and again, can lead to good, publishable results.

Generalisability

We have already mentioned the importance of having a representative sample, whether of people or material in your study. As we said, if your sample is representative of the population you are interested in (student drinkers, or the British or Irish press, or whatever), then your findings can be *generalised* to other similar student drinkers, or other examples of the press. Again, we say more about sampling and how to do it effectively in Chapter 4.

The 'wh' questions: what, why, where, when, how and with whom?

In the box below, we give an example of an exercise which we have carried out with every group of students we have worked with in teaching research methods. Students are required to answer these questions at the beginning of the course, and they can find them quite tough. This can be done in collaboration with other students or individually. Discussing with others can be a help in formulating ideas and tightening up definitions.

STEPS FOR DRAWING UP A DISSERTATION OR RESEARCH PROJECT PROPOSAL: THE 'WH' QUESTIONS

TOPIC

1. WHAT?
Is the topic you would like to study?

2. WHAT
Do you want to know about it?

OUTCOME 1:

RESEARCH QUESTION
AND
RESEARCH HYPOTHESIS
Formulate your topic of inquiry in BOTH ways.

2. WHY?
Are you interested in it?
Does it matter?

3. WHO?

Else has done similar research? (mention some readings, at least three citations at this stage, of prior literature in the field)

Would be interested in knowing about it?

Will you do it with? (if you want to do empirical fieldwork, interviews or surveys).

METHOD

4. HOW

Will you do it? (The method question)

5. WHERE

Will you do it?

6. WHO

Will you do it with?

OUTCOME 2: Description of at least TWO appropriate methods for your research question and why you think they are appropriate

5. WHAT (AGAIN)

Do you hope your study will add to the existing knowledge in your chosen field of inquiry?

OVERALL OUTCOME:

A two-page, 750–1,000 word dissertation proposal which includes:

- answers to all the above questions;
- a brief account of the process by which you arrived at them;
- an account of any remaining areas of uncertainty and how you might address these.

Group versus individual projects

Our final section in this introduction to formulating a research question and beginning to design a way of answering it concerns whether you work as an individual or in a group. We have worked with students under both conditions: on individual dissertation projects with BA, MA and PhD students and with groups of students in research methods classes. Sometimes, but perhaps not often enough, students carry out a dissertation project either in pairs or in a group, but generally because students have to be given an individual mark for a dissertation, and because dissertations carry quite a high proportion of marks on many courses, individual projects are more encouraged in educational courses than group ones. Nevertheless, in the real world, social science research is carried out in teams, with groups of people working together, and it is valuable experience for students to learn how to design and carry out a project in conjunction with other people.

Steps in carrying out group projects

In the kinds of research described in this book – questionnaire surveys and content analysis – it is quite difficult for students to conduct all the work required to collect large numbers of samples and to analyse them individually. When only a short time is available – as in the postgraduate workshops we taught, where we had only four weeks for each workshop – it was essential that students divided the labour and worked in groups. In this case, students had to carry out the following steps:

1. They had to get themselves into groups of four or five people who were interested in pursuing broadly similar research questions. Sometimes lecturing staff prefer to put people into groups and not allow students to choose their team-mates, but, while this is usually necessary with children, this is less ideal for adults. Autonomy of judgement is to be encouraged in research, as are good working relationships within a group.
2. They had to decide on a research question collectively, using the above 'wh questions' exercise.
3. They had to divide the labour of the project, e.g. one person was responsible for typing and printing questionnaires; another was responsible for entering data into the computer program; a third was responsible for designing a PowerPoint (or other) presentation of the findings; all were responsible for collecting data – for example, each person had to find twenty respondents for their questionnaire, or each person had to code and analyse a quarter of the sample material in a content analysis.
4. In formal presentations to the rest of the class, which were marked and assessed, each student had to make a contribution of some kind. We have also used procedures where students contributed

a proportion of the marking by carrying out a self-assessment of the project in their final report.

5. Each student had to write up their own version of the project in the final research report, which was given an individual mark. Thus the introduction/literature review and the final discussion of the results in each report had to be the work of each individual. This way, less hardworking individuals could not benefit from the extra work of others, and conversely, good and conscientious students were not 'carrying' those who were less conscientious.

In our next chapter we leave the practicalities of devising and setting up a research project and turn in more detail to the all-important question of *method*.

CHAPTER 3

Choosing a Method

This chapter deals with the **'how'** question: the methodology of your research project and some basic elements and terms of quantitative research design. As we pointed out in the last chapter, the research question you formulate will largely determine the methods you choose, so it's important to be clear and precise about what your question is. A further key ingredient for validity in research design is to have *more than one method* to answer your research question; questionnaires using number coding should also include space for qualitative information in the person's own words, such as a question at the end asking:

'Do you have any other comments?'

and some space for people to write these comments. These comments have a dual function: to act as a further reliability check on the numerical information in the questionnaire answers; and to provide extra, more nuanced and personalised details to augment or explain this information more clearly. Approaching a conclusion from two different points in this way is sometimes called **triangulation.** An example from our own research is described below.

In some research on children and television drama carried out by Máire Messenger Davies and colleagues at the London College of Printing for the BBC (*Dear BBC*, 2001, pp. 175–6), 1,332 children in different parts of the UK, aged between six and thirteen, were asked in their questionnaires to say whether they agreed, disagreed or weren't sure about the following statement:

'I want more programmes for children my age.'

The proportion agreeing to this statement – 70 per cent – was the highest level of agreement of anything we asked in the questionnaire. In the case of 9–12-year-olds, the pre-teens, the proportion agreeing was even higher: 74 per cent. Clearly, 'my age' was an important concept for children in determining how they saw themselves and other children, and how they formed their tastes, and we wanted to know more about the reasons behind this. The research team got more insight into this finding from some of the free comments on the questionnaire, for example this eleven-year-old boy from Cardiff:

> I would like to see a lot of drama on telly. I hate to see too much children's cartoons because they're on every day of the week, even on the weekend. There should be more interesting programmes for children that have grown out of cartoons. (quoted in *Dear BBC*, p. 39)

This comment drew attention to two key features of children's attitudes to 'age', which we could not have obtained from the purely quantitative data in the rest of the questionnaire: first, it appears that, for children, there are specific genres associated with different age groups. Cartoons for this boy are clearly 'children's' and he does not include himself in this category. One of the questions on the questionnaire was:

'Cartoons are only for little children'

and there was a range of responses to this, with the oldest group (11–13-year-olds) disagreeing most strongly. The research team interpreted this to mean that these pre-teens were dissociating themselves from 'little children', rather than that they didn't like cartoons as a genre. This boy's comment supports our interpretation.

The second revealing comment made by this boy was his use of the term 'grown out of'. It implied that, for him, one reason why children's tastes change is not that they are cultural and imposed by society, but developmental, an unavoidable part of growing up. This view was an example of the way in which children show awareness of academic debates, such as the relative importance of genetics versus social conditioning in shaping people's behaviour and tastes. Children themselves are going through the process of 'growing up' and are in a particularly favourable position to comment on it.

In the qualitative discussion tasks carried out afterwards with small groups, even more insight into this answer emerged when the children were asked to create a schedule of programmes for other children. 'Age' came up repeatedly as a reason for including, or excluding, programme titles, for example:

> 'We tried to think of the age of the children [in our schedule]. *Live and Kicking* was for our age and *999* and *The X Files* was for older people and older children.' (Girl, 9, Inner London primary school)

So the qualitative information supported and enhanced the quantitative information; it allowed the children to expand on what they meant by 'age' and what they thought was suitable entertainment for different age groups. Having this information in the children's own words also meant that there was some lively and readable material to give to our clients, the BBC, and to the general readers of Máire Messenger Davies's book, *Dear BBC*. But the qualitative information would not have been enough on its own, because it came only from small groups of articulate children, not from the whole sample of over 1,300 children. It was not **generalisable**.

Focus groups

Another way of providing back-up information for a questionnaire is to carry out a **focus group** – a small group discussion with some of the questionnaire respondents. We did this in conjunction with a questionnaire given to visitors to the West Yorkshire Playhouse in September 2001, in which we were investigating the relationship between popular culture, such as cult TV series (*Star Trek* in this case), and 'high' culture, such as live theatre. The theatre was running a J. B. Priestley (local author) festival and had revived his play, not performed since 1960, *Johnson over Jordan*, starring Patrick Stewart. Stewart was the star of *Star Trek: The Next Generation*, as well as being a distinguished stage actor.[1] We asked the theatre-goers to respond to the following statements:

I go to the theatre	6–12 times a year	2–5 times a year	Once a year	Less than once a year	Never

I go to the West Yorkshire Playhouse	First time visit	Rarely	Sometimes	Often	Very often

---

[1] M. M. Davies and R. E. Pearson (2003) 'Stardom and Distinction: Patrick Stewart as an Agent of Cultural Mobility: A study of Theatre and Film Audiences in New York City', in M. Barker and T. Austin (eds.), *Contemporary Hollywood Stardom*, London: Arnold, pp. 167–86; M. M. Davies and R. E. Pearson 'To boldly bestride the narrow world like a colossus: Shakespeare, *Star Trek* and the European TV Market', in I. Bondebjerg and P. Golding (eds.), *European Culture and the Media: Changing Media Changing Europe*, Vol. 1, Bristol: Intellect Books, pp. 65–90: R. E. Pearson and M. M. Davies (2005) 'Class Acts? Public and Private Values and the Cultural Habits of Theatre-goers', in S. Livingstone (ed.), *Audiences and Publics*, Bristol: Intellect Books.

When we analysed the answers we found a surprisingly high number of infrequent theatre-goers. The questionnaire responses didn't give us any insight into *why* these infrequent theatre-goers came to this particular play, although we had a hunch (hypothesis) that they were there because they liked the leading actor, Patrick Stewart, and that they might have been fans of *Star Trek: the Next Generation*. Our focus group discussions gave us support for this hypothesis – for instance, these comments from 41-year-old Steven, a postman driver: 'The main reason I came is that I heard such good reviews and I wanted to see Patrick Stewart . . . I'm not a regular theatre-goer.'

The qualitative discussions, as qualitative discussions often do, also gave us some information that we hadn't asked for, but were valuable for our research all the same: an extra insight into the powerful impact that live theatre can have on someone who isn't used to it. This is Steven again:

> I was tired, because I'd just come off nights and I'd had just about four hours' sleep in the previous two weeks and every scene I thought was fascinating, you know. Every one was an eye-opener to me. I didn't get bored at all and didn't fall asleep or anything.

This was valuable information for the theatre marketing team, and also for us in terms of our interest in people's cultural tastes generally, and how and why they change – information that we could not have obtained just from the questionnaire answers.

The building blocks of survey research: a 'baby questionnaire'

We are now going to backtrack a little from the more complex, real-world examples of questionnaire research which we have carried out, to a much simpler example: a training exercise on how to design, code, administer and analyse a short questionnaire, using SPSS (Statistical Package for the Social Sciences). We call this our 'baby questionnaire' in that it is extremely simple, basic and minimal in the questions it asks. To pursue the baby analogy, it enables students to learn to walk before they try to run.

Questionnaires are one of the most powerful research tools; they are the most economical way of collecting a lot of information from a large number of people in a relatively short time. This brief exercise is an introduction to basic questionnaire design and analysis using SPSS. Note that this little 'baby questionnaire', even though it has only five questions in it, has the two essential ingredients of all good questionnaires:

1. A 'demographic' section: information about the person filling it in.
2. An information section: the questions you are interested in for your project, in this case a hypothetical survey on political attitudes.

QUANTITATIVE RESEARCH WITH SPSS: 'BABY QUESTIONNAIRE' EXERCISE

* *

ATTITUDES TO THE EUROPEAN UNION QUESTIONNAIRE

Please circle or tick the answer that applies to you:

ABOUT YOU (*using multiple-choice*)

1. I am   Male/Female

2. My status is: Undergraduate
                              Postgraduate

3. I am enrolled on: BA
                              MA
                              PhD
                              Other (please specify) (*using post-coding*)

YOUR VIEWS ON THE EU (*using the Likert scale*)

4. Britain's membership of the European Union is a good thing.

1. Strongly disagree   2. Disagree   3. Not sure   4. Agree   5. Strongly agree

5. The UK Government is doing a good job.

1. Strongly disagree   2. Disagree   3. Not sure   4. Agree   5. Strongly agree

Any other comments? (*using qualitative data*)

Thank you for your help.

Questionnaire sections

1. Demographics

All questionnaires require a section in which respondents give information about themselves. These characteristics are called **demographics**. People's demographic characteristics can make an important difference to how they answer your questions. What exactly you want to know about them will – again, as always – depend on your specific research question. In our 'baby' example we've used just two: age and sex (gender).

Age and sex

Whatever your research question, it is always wise to have information about the two basic human characteristics of age and sex/gender. This is because they apply to everybody, whereas the other characteristics on the list may not (e.g. children may not have an income; not everybody is educated; even place of origin may not be relevant or known). Also, past research with human beings, as well as your personal experience, indicate that these two characteristics are highly likely to *make a difference* to the ways in which people answer: the different responses people give, as well as their different demographic characteristics, are called **variables**; we will say more about the more technical meanings of this term later. For the time being it's sufficient to note that the common-sense meaning of 'vary' is relevant to defining this term; research asking about people's characteristics is based on the assumption that people vary.[2]

Other demographic characteristics include:

- **income;**
- **occupation;**
- **nationality;**
- **ethnicity/race;**
- **education;**
- **place of origin;**
- **religion.**

---

[2] Or, strictly speaking, using the null hypothesis, we can make the assumption that people *don't* vary and that any differences we observe between people are due to chance, until the differences become so marked that they would appear to show a genuinely *significant* distinction, as measured by statistical tests.

Depending on your research question you may want to know about any or all of the above characteristics. For instance, you may well think that 'religion' will affect the way people answer questions about news from Northern Ireland or from Saudi Arabia, because Ireland and the Middle East are areas of religious conflict. If we take the student example we used in the last chapter, a researcher carrying out research into supposed journalistic bias in the reporting of Northern Ireland would be justified in thinking that the journalists' religion could be relevant to their reporting. A question about religion therefore needs to be included in a questionnaire given to journalists. Any of these categories can be potentially controversial, but if people do not wish to answer questions about themselves, they do not have to. You can include the category 'do not wish to respond' as part of your list of potential responses, and then these people can be distinguished from those who couldn't be bothered to respond or forgot the question.

If you think that religion isn't relevant to the questions you are asking, then don't include it. The same goes for income or occupation: if you are surveying students, these questions are unlikely to be relevant, so leave them out. However, in the case of our theatre-goers at the West Yorkshire Playhouse, questions about income and education were relevant to our interest in people's cultural tastes and how they might vary and change, so they were included.

2. An information/attitude section
In this section people answer the questions you are especially interested in for your research project. For the purposes of our exercise, we have included just two: a question about people's attitudes to the European Union and one about their attitudes to the UK domestic situation. In a student study about alcohol consumption which we are using as an example of a student project, there were fourteen questions about students' attitudes to drinking. In the BBC study about children's views on television drama, the research team included fourteen questions asking their views about various aspects of TV storytelling. We will say more about the optimum number of questions, how they should be worded and how they should be laid out in our chapter on questionnaire design (Chapter 6). But no matter how long and diverse the questions in a questionnaire are, it will still consist of the same two basic sections: demographics about the people answering, and information about

their responses to your particular research question. Your assumption will be that the answers given in the first section (age, sex, income level or whatever) will *make a difference* to the answers given in the second section. This assumption can be tested, very straightforwardly, through the SPSS analysis, as we shall see.

3. Cultural consumption/tastes

In the case of media research, a sub-section to your demographic section may be desirable, asking about people's media consumption and tastes. For instance, in the West Yorkshire study, we asked people how often they watched particular television programmes and how often they went to the theatre. In the case of our student project about journalistic bias, the student might want to know how often people watched television news or how regularly they read a daily newspaper, and which news programmes and newspapers they used. The assumption is that being a regular theatre-goer or newspaper reader is likely *to make a difference* to how you answer questions about particular theatrical experiences or particular items in the news (see footnote 2).

Questionnaire instruments

In the 'baby questionnaire', you will see that we have attached the following labels to the questions:

- **multiple-choice;**
- **post-coding;**
- **Likert scale;**
- **qualitative data.**

These are labels for the kinds of questions that most often occur in questionnaires; below we give a brief explanation of them. All, with the exception of qualitative data, are designed to make it easier for you to give the answers numerical *codings* and thus to analyse them statistically with SPSS.

Multiple-choice

Rather than ask people to say whether they are male and female (or to say how old they are, or how much they earn), it is simpler to give them some options and ask them to choose one: in the case of age, you may use age categories, as we did in the West Yorkshire project:

Please **circle** the appropriate category, e.g. if you are 28-years-old, circle 26–35:

Age (Years)	0–10	11–16	17–25	26–35	36–45	46–55	56–65	65+

You can do this with other kinds of questions, for instance questions about media tastes: rather than ask people what newspapers they read, give them a list of newspapers and ask them to circle the ones they usually read, or the one they read most often. The preference for multiple-choice questions in research is based on the long-established finding in psychological studies of memory that 'cued recall' (when people are given prompts to answer a question) is a better way of finding out what they remember than 'free recall' (when they are asked to describe what they saw or what they read).

Post-coding

Having said that, sometimes you *do* want people to give their own answers, especially when you cannot be sure what those answers might be. For example, in our West Yorkshire Playhouse study, we had a hunch that many people came to the theatre to see Patrick Stewart, but we were not sure that we were right and we did not know what other reasons people might have had for coming. So we could not have constructed an accurate multiple-choice list for this question. We also did not want to prompt them with a 'demand characteristic' by suggesting that 'Patrick Stewart' might be a 'right' answer. Instead, we gave them an open-ended question:

> **What was the main reason that you came to see this play today?**

Table 3.1 below shows the numbers of people who gave particular answers and these were all given 'value labels' under the variable label 'reason for coming'. So 'Patrick Stewart' was coded 1, J. B. Priestley coded 2, and so on. This table has been arranged in 'descending counts' so that you can see the most frequently mentioned reason at the top. It could also have been counted simply according to the order in which the values had been coded. This is shown in Table 3.2.

Table 3.1 Reasons for coming to the West Yorkshire Playhouse to see *Johnson over Jordan*, September 2001: 'Descending counts' (in order of 'votes cast') Main Reason For Coming*

		Frequency	Per cent	Valid per cent	Cumulative per cent
Valid	Patrick Stewart	264	27.5	30.3	30.3
	J.B. Priestley	136	14.2	15.6	45.9
	Friends/family/ partner	76	7.9	8.7	54.6
	Stewart + Priestley	68	7.1	7.8	62.4
	Interest in this production	37	3.9	4.2	66.6
	Curiosity/general interest	36	3.7	4.1	70.8
	Opportunity – tickets	31	3.2	3.6	74.3
	Recommendation	30	3.1	3.4	77.8
	Subscription/regular at WYP	22	2.3	2.5	80.3
	Publicity	20	2.1	2.3	82.6
	Interest in theatre	16	1.7	1.8	84.4
	Opportunity – holiday/ in the area	12	1.2	1.4	85.8
	Educational/study	11	1.1	1.3	87.0
	Opportunity – group travel	8	0.8	0.9	88.0
	Member of Priestley Society	8	0.8	0.9	88.9

Entertainment/ pleasure	7	0.7	0.8	89.7
Interested in this production + Stewart	5	0.5	0.6	90.3
Spur of the moment	5	0.5	0.6	90.8
Birthday present/ special occasion	5	0.5	0.6	91.4
Patrick Stewart + recommendation	4	0.4	0.5	91.9
Forced	4	0.4	0.5	92.3
Avril Clark	4	0.4	0.5	92.8
Shakespeare	3	0.3	0.3	93.1
Priestley + interest in this production	3	0.3	0.3	93.5
Free tickets + Patrick Stewart	3	0.3	0.3	93.8
Subscription + Priestley	3	0.3	0.3	94.2
Opportunity – production not often shown	2	0.2	0.2	94.4
Because of the actors	2	0.2	0.2	94.6
Good show	2	0.2	0.2	94.8
Jude Kelly + Stewart	2	0.2	0.2	95.1
Priestley + Stewart + theatre generally	2	0.2	0.2	95.3
Priestley Theatre +	2	0.2	0.2	95.5
Patrick Stewart + birthday present	2	0.2	0.2	95.8

* Table does not show all data.

Table 3.2 'Reason for coming' presented according to post-coding order

Main Reason For Coming*

		Frequency	Per cent	Valid Per cent	Cumulative Per cent
Valid	Patrick Stewart	264	27.5	30.3	30.3
	J.B. Priestley	136	14.2	15.6	45.9
	Stewart + Priestley	68	7.1	7.8	53.7
	Interest in theatre	16	1.7	1.8	55.5
	publicity	20	2.1	2.3	57.8
	Curiosity/general interest	36	3.7	4.1	61.9
	Opportunity – tickets	31	3.2	3.6	65.5
	Opportunity – group travel	8	0.8	0.9	66.4
	Friends/family/ partner	76	7.9	8.7	75.1
	Subscription/ regular at WYP	22	2.3	2.5	77.6
	Member of Priestley Society	8	0.8	0.9	78.6
	Opportunity – production not often shown	2	0.2	0.2	78.8
	Interested in performing art	1	0.1	0.1	78.9
	Recommendation	30	3.1	3.4	82.3

Interest in this production	37	3.9	4.2	86.6
Interest in theatre and interest in production	1	0.1	0.1	86.7
Because of the actors	2	0.2	0.2	86.9
Patrick Stewart + recommen-dation	4	0.4	0.5	87.4
Good show	2	0.2	0.2	87.6
Member of Kendall Theatre Club	1	0.1	0.1	87.7
To get a life	1	0.1	0.1	87.8
Educational/study	11	1.1	1.3	89.1
Interested in this production + Stewart	5	0.5	0.6	89.7
Shakespeare	3	0.3	0.3	90.0
Interest + Stewart	1	0.1	0.1	90.1
Jude Kelly + Stewart	2	0.2	0.2	90.4
Opportunity – holiday/in the area	12	1.2	1.4	91.7
Read the book	1	0.1	0.1	91.9
Priestley + stewart + theatre generally	2	0.2	0.2	92.1
Theatre + Priestley	2	0.2	0.2	92.3

* Table does not show all data.

From the answers we were able to construct a list of 'reasons', to each of which we gave a numerical coding. This list is shown in the tables 3.1 and 3.2 and is called 'post-coding' because you don't allocate the numbers until after you have the answers. We also gave people the option of giving their own answer in one of the questions in our 'baby questionnaire'. If they weren't enrolled on a BA, MA or PhD programme, we asked them to say what kind of course they were taking – Diploma, Foundation, or whatever, which could then be given a numerical 'post'- (or 'after') coding. We will say more about this when we get to the general question of coding below. Suffice to say here that it is possible to turn people's own words into numerical form when you have given them a 'free recall' question in a questionnaire, so you should not be afraid to give the occasional free-choice question.

Likert scale

This is probably the most widely used tool for assessing people's opinions in survey research: the five-point scale, stating a range of positions from strong disagreement to strong agreement with three points between. An example is given below:

'People should have to pay subscriptions for all television channels'

1	2	3	4	5
Strongly disagree	Disagree	Neutral	Agree	Strongly agree

The five-point scale is a robust way of allowing people to express variations in opinion or behaviour which provide meaningful answers to researchers about these variations. In the case of the question above, people who agree, or strongly agree, might be those with specialised interests, like sport, and we might also suppose that they earn more than other people because subscription isn't a problem for them. These assumptions can be checked with reference to their demographic information (their income) and to their media consumption (as in the question below). Those who disagree we might expect to be older and less familiar with multi-channel television – again, we can check this against the demographics. (And of course, our assumptions may be wrong, which is why we must test them.)

An alternative format for the Likert scale is to ask people how often they do something – for example, we might want to ask people who'd answered the question above about their viewing habits:

'I watch sports on television'

1	2	3	4	5
Never	Hardly ever	Sometimes	Often	Very often

We might expect there to be a relationship (*correlation*) between people who were in favour of subscription channels and people who watch sports often; thus, we could predict that those who circled 4 or 5 on the first question are more likely to circle 4 or 5 on the second. This can be checked with SPSS.

Statements not questions

There are two important points to note about the Likert scale. The first is the wording. These types of questions are never, in fact, questions; they are always statements. Rather than ask people 'Do you agree with subscription?' in which case the only possible answer is 'yes', or 'no', you give them options which enable them to express a range of agreement or disagreement. The same is true of people's behaviour or habits, which very rarely fall neatly into the 'always' or 'never' categories. The five-point scale provides a subtler and more nuanced way of evaluating people's habits and attitudes than simply asking 'yes' or 'no' questions; it allows people a range of choices rather than forcing them to give an answer which may not correspond exactly to what they really think, so in effect, they end up lying. It acknowledges the ambiguity and complexity of most people's attitudes and it has proved surprisingly revealing in the many studies in which it has been used.

The second point to note about the Likert scale is the numerical order. In both cases we give above, the scale represents a range, with one end of the scale being very negative and the other being very positive, with a range of feeling/experience going up the gradient in between: the numbers 1–5 have some relationship to what they are measuring in that they go from low to high, but it is a rough-and-ready relationship, rather than a very precisely accurate one. This is called '**ordinal**' measurement and we say more about it below.

So in our 'baby questionnaire', you can see that we have given two Likert scales in which people are asked to rate their attitudes to political issues on a scale of 1–5. In a proper research project, of course, we would give a lot more Likert statements.

Qualitative data

We have already talked about qualitative and quantitative information. The 'any further comments' space on the questionnaire allows people to say something in their own words, such as, 'I think the domestic situation is OK, but this doesn't mean I approve of everything the Government does.' This can be used to support, or further enhance or explain, the information you get from the other questionnaire answers. At this point, we should also say something about the term 'data', which we have been using and will use a lot more. 'Data' comes from the Latin verb 'dare' (pronounced dah-ray), meaning 'to give'; 'datum' means 'given' and 'data' is the plural of this, meaning a number of things that have been given, in other words, all the information derived from your research procedures. Data (always a plural word) can be qualitative or quantitative, as we have said.

Coding

- **Variable labels**
- **Value labels**
- **Nominal data**
- **Ordinal data**
- **Interval data**

We now need to turn our 'baby questionnaire' into a form of information that the computer program can understand: we need to code each piece of information and give it a numerical value. We do this using the terminology (language) of the SPSS program.

Each question is called a '**variable**' and, in the first column of the SPSS table, it has to be given a short **variable label**, no longer than six letters.

Nominal data

Within each variable, there are, as we've said, a number of options, or *values*, and each option/value also has to be given a numerical coding. In the case of 'variable 1', 'gender', there are two options/values, male and female: we can use the terms 'male' and 'female' as **'value labels'**.

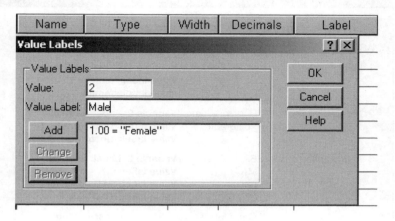

We can code male as 1 and female as 2, or vice versa; it makes no difference. This kind of number coding is called **nominal data**. From the Latin for 'name', nomen, 'nominal data' means that the numbers in this case are simply names, like Fred and Alice. Switching them round and making female 1 and male 2, has no significance: 1 is not superior to 2, nor is 2 twice as good as 1. Other sorts of nominal data could be, for example, occupations: your questionnaire might have a list of six different professions: medicine, law, teaching, business, social work, architect. They would be coded 1–6 but it wouldn't matter in which order; calling social work 5 or 3 has no numerical significance at all. It is simply a label.

Ordinal data

In the case of variable 2 in our sample questionnaire, 'status', there are also two options: 'undergrad' and 'postgrad'. These too can be coded 1 and 2, but in this case, although the data could be seen as nominal, we might argue that 2 is higher than 1 because a postgrad is at a more advanced stage of education than an undergrad. In the case of this little questionnaire it doesn't really matter very much. But if we were conducting a study in which people's level of education is relevant to our main research questions, it *would* matter.

ATTITUDES TO THE EUROPEAN UNION QUESTIONNAIRE

Please circle or tick the answer that applies to you:

ABOUT YOU (*using multiple-choice*)

1. I am	Male / Female:	**Variable 1: Label: 'gender'** **value label: 'male' – 1** **value label: 'female' – 2**
2. My status is:	Undergraduate: Postgraduate	**Variable 2: Label: 'status'** **Value label: 'undergrad' – 1** **Value label: 'postgrad' – 2**
3. I am enrolled on:	BA MA PhD	**Variable 3: Label: 'degree'** **Value label: 'BA' – 1** **Value label: 'MA' – 2** **Value label: 'PhD' – 3**

Other (please specify) (*using post-coding*)

YOUR VIEWS ON THE EU (*using the Likert scale*)

4. Britain's membership of the European   **Variable 4: Label: 'eumemb'**
   Union is a good thing: **Value labels: as in the scale**

1. Strongly disagree   2. Disagree   3. Not sure   4. Agree   5. Strongly agree

5. The UK Government is doing a good job. **Variable 5: Label: 'ukgov'**
                                             Value labels: as in the scale

1. Strongly disagree   2. Disagree   3. Not sure   4. Agree   5. Strongly agree

Any other comments? (*using qualitative data*)

Let's say we were interested in people's attitudes to politics generally; we might have a Likert scale question stating:

'It's important for everybody to vote in national elections.'

People who 'strongly agree', we might assume, are more likely to be highly educated. (Again, we might be wrong.) So we would arrange our options in the 'status' question in *order* of educational level to see whether the higher up the order a person is, the more strongly they feel about voting. In coding the variable 'status', we could do this:

1. 'secondary education to age sixteen';
2. 'sixth form/further education';
3. 'BA degree';

4   'MA degree';
5. 'PhD'.

In this case the numbers *do* represent a range from low to high and are not just names; in this case we would call the numbers **ordinal data** because they constitute an order, or rank, which represents real differences in level and length of educational experience. People coded 5 are at a more advanced stage in their education than people coded 1, so we might expect there to be a numerical relationship between higher codings (4 and 5) on 'educational status' and higher levels of agreement (4 and 5) about the importance of political issues.

Ordinal data, that is, rankings from low to high, require different sorts of statistical analysis from nominal data, and the computer program needs to know this, hence the column at the end of the SPSS table asking for information about the kind of data you are using for each question, or variable.

The final two questions on our 'baby questionnaire' are Likert scales, asking people's opinions on the European Union and the UK Government. Likert scales, too, are ordinal data – they represent a range of opinion from one extreme to the other. This is not the same as saying 'from low to high' so there is a sense in which a five-point Likert measure of disagreement/agreement doesn't rise straightforwardly from 1 to 5. Strong disagreement is a strong measure, so coding it as 1 might be seen as misleading. Nevertheless, for the purpose of most attitude questions, which are only rough estimates of people's feelings, the 1–5 scale can be assumed to correspond broadly to a range of feeling from negative to positive.

Interval data
The final kind of data that is identified in an SPSS data file is called '**scale**' or '**interval**' data. In our sample questionnaire (above) we don't have any examples of interval data, and they don't turn up that often in survey research of the kind we are describing. (They are more likely to turn up in content analysis; see Chapter 7.) However, we could have included an example of interval data under the label (variable) 'age'. Rather than give people a range of options (values) for 'age', as we did in West Yorkshire, we could have asked them simply to give their age in years: 12, 15, 33, 41, 65 or whatever. This kind of numbering is called **interval data**. Sorting out the difference

between interval and ordinal data has proved to be one of the most difficult problems for students that we have encountered in our experience of teaching quantitative methods. *But it is absolutely essential that these distinctions are understood.*

Is the difference 'one'?

The clearest way of identifying interval, as distinct from ordinal, data is to ask: *What is the difference between each point on the scale?* In the case of age, what is the difference between one year and two years; between two years and three years; between 22 and 23 years? If the answer is *always 'one'*, then you are dealing with interval data. In other words, you are dealing with the kinds of numbers you are most used to for counting in everyday life; the difference between £1 and £2, between five oranges and six oranges, and so on: the difference is always 'one'.

In the case of the ordinal codes 1–5 which we allocated to different levels of education in the example above, we can see that asking about the difference between each point on the scale is not such a meaningful question: the difference between point 1 on the scale, 'secondary education to age sixteen', and point 2, 'sixth form/further education', is not an exact numerical difference. The two points simply represent a higher and lower level of education. However, if we had asked people to say how many *years* they had spent in full-time education, *then* we would have had an interval scale: the difference between six years and seven years, or nine years and ten years, is always one. Such a question however, would not be particularly meaningful if we want to know – as we do in this case – how well qualified these people are. We need to know what 'level' they have reached, not just how long they spent sitting at a desk. Here, an ordinal scale is more useful.

Test question

And, in this hypothetical case, if we needed to code which school they went to, as Davies et al. did with the nineteen schools in the BBC study discussed above, with School A being coded 1, School B being coded 2, School H being coded 3, School Y being coded 4, and so on, what sort of data would that be?

See if you can work it out.

Postscript: post-coding

In question/variable 3 in our 'baby questionnaire', labelled 'degree', we had three options/values: 1, BA, 2, MA, 3 PhD and an 'other' option. In this case we need to use numbers from 4 onwards to post-code any answers that people put in the 'other' section. Let us say that the first person answering the 'other' option put 'Postgrad diploma'; we would include 'diploma' as another option/value, and code it 4. If the next person put 'Foundation' we would code it 5. And so on, in this free comment section, we would go on allocating numbers for each new course mentioned.

Another test question: post-coding

If a second person, in addition to the first person, put 'Foundation' in the 'other' section, how would you code this answer?

If the next person after this one put 'exchange student, Erasmus programme' how would you code it?

In our West Yorkshire study, there were a number of free-choice questions, such as the one we mentioned above:

'What was the main reason you came to the theatre today?'

With each new answer we received–

'regular subscriber',
'free tickets',
'birthday treat'

– we gave it a numerical coding. The first reason in the first questionnaire we looked at was:

'I came to see Patrick Stewart'

so we coded 'Patrick Stewart' 1 in our 'reason' variable. Each time one of our questionnaires showed that the main reason this person came to the play was 'Patrick Stewart', their answer to this question was coded 1. There were sixty-seven reasons altogether, including combined reasons coded, 1–67. As you can see, with post-coding there can be a lot of options/values and you go on adding numbers until you have no more new reasons being added. This is fine; the program will handle them with no problem. For instance, one of our questions was:

'What is your favourite television programme?'

and people came up with 206 different titles. They were coded 1–206. By asking the SPSS program to count how many of the values under variable/question 29 'favourite TV' were labelled '1' or '201' or whatever, we could then check to see how many people had 'voted' for each title.

Missing values

What happens if someone does not answer one of the questions? You can't leave the coding sheet blank, nor can you put '0', because zero is a real numerical value which you may need; you need to tell the computer program that the answer to the question is 'missing' and this is usually done by putting in an 'impossible' number, such as 99, or 999. This is a number that won't be used in your coding because you don't have that many questions or values.

What do the answers look like?

The spreadsheets (pp. 55–6). show two versions of some answers to our 'baby questionnaire' – data from twenty imaginary people who 'filled it in'. The first version shows the verbal version of this information; the second version shows the number coding. In modern versions of SPSS, in which you can see the verbal versions, it is much easier for students to understand what they are dealing with. In earlier versions, there were no words, only number codings: you can imagine how baffling these columns and grids of 1's, 5's, 3's, and 99's were. However, we managed!

In our classroom exercises, we give these data to our students and get them to answer some simple questions using the program. We will not be asking you to do this at this stage. In Chapters 10 and 11, we will discuss in more detail how to analyse and interpret the data you have collected and coded with your questionnaires. Meanwhile, we continue with the next important stage of setting up a research project: selecting a **sample** to work with. This can be either a human sample – people you want to answer your questionnaire – or, in the case of content analysis, it will be a sample of media material. Appropriate sampling is absolutely essential in ensuring external validity for a research project, and as always, the sample you select will depend on your research question.

Spreadsheet 1

	sex	status	degree	eumemb	domsit
1	Female	Postgraduate	MA	Strongly Agree	Good
2	Female	Undergraduate	BA	Strongly Agree	Very Good
3	Female	Undergraduate	BA	Strongly Agree	Very Good
4	Female	Undergraduate	BA	Strongly Agree	Good
5	Male	Undergraduate	Other	Somewhat Agree	Very Good
6	Female	Postgraduate	PhD	Strongly Agree	Good
7	Male	Undergraduate	BA	Somewhat Agree	Neither Good nor Bad
8	Male	Undergraduate	BA	Somewhat Agree	Very Bad
9	Male	99.00	MA	Somewhat Disagree	Very Bad
10	Male	Postgraduate	Other	Strongly Agree	Good
11	Female	Postgraduate	Other	Somewhat Agree	Good
12	Male	Undergraduate	BA	Somewhat Agree	Neither Good nor Bad
13	Male	Postgraduate	PhD	Strongly Agree	Good
14	Female	Postgraduate	PhD	Somewhat Disagree	Bad
15	Male	Undergraduate	BA	Strongly Agree	Good
16	Male	Postgraduate	PhD	Somewhat Disagree	Good ·
17	Female	Undergraduate	BA	Somewhat Agree	Good
18	Male	Undergraduate	Other	Neutral	Neither Good nor Bad
19	Female	Postgraduate	MA	Strongly Agree	Very Good
20	Male	Postgraduate	PhD	Strongly Agree	Good

	sex	status	degree	eumemb	domsit
			Spreadsheet 2		
1	1.00	2.00	2.00	1.00	2.00
2	1.00	1.00	1.00	1.00	1.00
3	1.00	1.00	1.00	1.00	1.00
4	1.00	1.00	1.00	1.00	2.00
5	2.00	1.00	4.00	2.00	1.00
6	1.00	2.00	3.00	1.00	2.00
7	2.00	1.00	1.00	2.00	3.00
8	2.00	1.00	1.00	2.00	5.00
9	2.00	99.00	2.00	4.00	5.00
10	2.00	2.00	4.00	1.00	2.00
11	1.00	2.00	4.00	2.00	2.00
12	2.00	1.00	1.00	2.00	3.00
13	2.00	2.00	3.00	1.00	2.00
14	1.00	2.00	3.00	4.00	4.00
15	2.00	1.00	1.00	1.00	2.00
16	2.00	2.00	3.00	4.00	2.00
17	1.00	1.00	1.00	2.00	2.00
18	2.00	1.00	4.00	3.00	3.00
19	1.00	2.00	2.00	1.00	1.00
20	2.00	2.00	3.00	1.00	2.00

PART TWO

EXECUTION: 'DOING IT'

CHAPTER 4

Sampling

The question of sampling is absolutely central in making sure that your project is **externally valid** (see p. 25) External validity means that the findings of your study can be applied more widely than just to your particular project – that is, they can be generalised. This is possible because you have taken every precaution to make sure that the people you have surveyed, or the media material you have selected to analyse, are *representative* of the group of people, or of the media material, you are primarily interested in.

For example, if you are doing a study about young girls' attitudes to body shape and the possible influence of advertising on their attitudes, you need to be sure that the young girls you include in your study are *typical* of the young girls as a whole at whom the advertising campaign is aimed. (Think about how you might find out what the *demographics* of this market might be.) Similarly, if you want to study the advertising material itself as well as the people it is aimed at, you need to make sure that the examples of advertising you select are generally typical of advertising aimed at young girls.

Having said this, with student projects, it is not always possible in the short time available, and with limited resources, to ensure that you have a truly representative sample of the whole population you are interested in. There are two basic ways round this, which we will say more about later:

1. Choose a topic – as with the example of student drinking habits mentioned on page 25 – where the people you want to study will be easily available, as in a university environment. 'Student drinkers' are obviously easier to sample than a huge, vague category like 'young people'.
2. Choose a sampling method where full representativeness is less of a crucial requirement. More details of these different sampling methods are given below.

Principles of sampling: key terms

The following are some key terms to understand the principles of sampling.

1. Population

This is the group from which the sample is drawn and which it represents. This need not be people, although we usually use the term to apply to people; it could be, for example, all TV sitcoms or a time period (e.g. Davies and Corbett's [1997] analysis of children's broadcasting output in the UK between 1991 and 1996)[1] or, as above, all advertising aimed at young females.

In the case of a survey of people, a population is everyone you are concerned with, e.g.:

- all the citizens in a country;
- all the PR professionals working in health care;
- all the people who read a certain newspaper;
- all students in your department;
- all MA students in your department.

Once again, you can see that the nature of the 'population' that you select for your study is derived from specific research questions. For the purpose of the national census, which needs to find out what everybody in the country is and does, the 'population' has to be 'all citizens'. For the purpose of looking at people's attitudes to the redesigned *Guardian*, the population has to be 'all *Guardian* readers'. If you are doing a survey of MA students' satisfaction with the technical resources available to them in the school (as one group of our MA students managed to do in a four-week workshop), 'all MA students in the department' is the population from which you will draw your sample. Even when you've reduced your 'population' to a specific group, unless you are doing a census, you still will not be able to question everybody in that population. You will need to select a **sample** from these populations.

---

[1] M. M. Davies and B. Corbett (1997) *Children's Television in Britain: An Enquiry for the Broadcasting Standards Commission*. London: Broadcasting Standards Commission.

2. Census

A census is a counting exercise which involves *everybody* (or every item) in the population. The national census is carried out in the UK every ten years, and every single person in the country, including children, is included in this survey; hence no sampling is involved.

3. Sample

For most research it is not practicable (or necessary) to count every single person. For most research, a sample is chosen from the population of interest to the project. A sample is a subgroup which is typical of the population as a whole. As we've said, sampling is necessary first, because it is not possible to ask everyone, for reasons of both cost and time; and second, for statistical reasons which we will not go into here, surveying everyone is not necessary: in a well-designed study, once you have a sufficiently large sample to cover all the ground of your research question (e.g. enough of each demographic subgroup), you will not get more reliable results statistically if you go on adding to the numbers in your sample.

It is possible to get a good idea of the population as a whole from a well-constructed sample. For example, the television ratings in the UK are based on a sample of only around 4,000 households in the whole country. Making the sample larger would not make the analysis of viewing figures any more reliable for reasons to do with statistical margins of error. (If you are interested in the precise reasons for this, and the mathematical analysis of it, see Chapter 14 of Wimmer and Dominick.)

4. Ways of sampling

(i) Random or probability sampling

With this most rigorous form of sampling every member of the population has an equal chance of being sampled. This is mainly used in large-scale quantitative surveys where having a representative sample is essential to provide results which can be generalised to a population at large. This is particularly necessary for governmental and policy research, where the findings of the survey could determine, for instance, the distribution of health care resources, or new housing. In random sampling the units (or people) are selected by chance and every unit has an equal likelihood of being selected. This may seem counterintuitive but in fact, this way of doing things (like putting a lot of numbers into a giant drum, rotating it and pulling out a number without looking at it, as in a lottery) is much the fairest way of selecting truly representative samples.

Types of random sampling

Random sampling can be done in a number of ways.

Systematic

- Number the entire population for example, 150 MA students.
- Depending on your research question (e.g. how many demographic subgroups you want to include), decide your sample size, for example, fifty.
- Work out an interval for picking your fifty out of the 150, for example every third student in the list.
- Start at random (e.g. by closing your eyes and pointing to a name) then use every third name until you have fifty.

Stratified

This is similar to the method described above, but the population is divided into particular groups (gender, age, nationality). Thus your population list may be divided into two lists of seventy-five males and seventy-five females and you sample each list randomly until you have twenty-five of each. You then subdivide the two lists into age groups to ensure you have sufficient numbers of, say under- and over-thirties (assuming age is relevant to your research question). As you can see, if you are going to subdivide your sample into particular demographic subgroups, your subgroups will become smaller and smaller the more categories you include, until the sample size for these subgroups cannot be seen as reliably representative. For instance twenty-five females, split equally into under- and over-thirties will give you only twelve or thirteen people in each group. If you want to look at four age categories, you will get only six or so people in each age and gender subgroup. The more demographic subgroups you divide your sample into, the larger your sample needs to be: another argument for keeping your research question and research design simple – for example, looking in detail only at the differences between *two* groups (males and females; or action adventure films versus romantic comedies).

Students sometimes want to make more complex comparisons between more than two or three groups of variables and this is possible using different forms of **multivariate analysis**, including a form of **multiple correlation** (see Chapter 10) called **multiple regression**. This analyses all demographic (and other) variables together, and works out which of them, and which combinations of them, make the biggest, or smallest, contribution to the overall results. However, we are not going to talk about multivariate analysis in this book, because, for the purpose of teaching research techniques and setting assessment exercises for Humanities students, such techniques have not been necessary for the kinds of questions they want to ask. Again, we recommend an SPSS handbook if you want to know more about these techniques. The SPSS 'help' facility within the program may also assist you, although in our experience students usually need to have access to flesh-and-blood teachers or fellow students when trying to navigate software help programs.

Quota

In this case, you decide what characteristics you want (how many males/females; how many of different age groups). Again, this decision depends on your research question. If gender differences are important, you need to make sure of having sufficiently balanced numbers of males and females in your sample, so you need to go on sampling names from the list, or add to the list, until you have this balance. When you split your population into males and females, you may find that you have very few females. If gender is important to your research question, you may need to recruit more females to your sample. Or you can carry out a statistical procedure known as '**weighting**' when you get to your data analysis stage. We advise you not to attempt advanced statistical procedures when carrying out simple student projects on a research methods course. For a MA or PhD dissertation, more advanced statistics may be necessary and feasible. In this case a good statistical chapter like the one in Wimmer and Dominick, or a text explaining the workings of SPSS, such as Andy Field (2005) *Discovering Statistics Using SPSS* (London, Thousand Oaks and Delhi: Sage), can be referred to. It would also be a good idea to enrol in a statistical research methods workshop offered by your university or college, although in our experience statistical training offered as a generic course or module, for instance in a multidisciplinary Graduate School, often does not take into account the particular needs, questions and interests of Humanities, Media and Cultural Studies students.

Quota sampling is typical of pollsters who may stop you on the street and ask if you belong to a particular group (journalism, advertising and so on) so that they can get the necessary representative percentage of different professional groups into their sample.

Student projects cannot usually use large, randomised, scientifically representative samples, because getting these involves gaining access to official records of households and then approaching these households, which is not possible for students conducting short-term projects. However, there are a number of other forms of sampling which students can adapt for their purposes. We list these ways below.

(ii) Non-probability (non-random) sampling
There are several kinds of non-random sampling, which is more often used in qualitative methods and in small-scale student projects which lack the time and resources to construct a full-scale, socially representative sample. These are:

- **Volunteer samples**: This is the kind of sample produced, for example, by magazine polls in which readers are invited to fill in a questionnaire in the magazine and send it in. The people who volunteer may be quite untypical of the readership as a whole or the population at large. Thus, even though quite large numbers may be involved, with thousands of respondents, this method is unscientific and unreliable. Pilot studies often use volunteers (friends and relatives who are willing to help) and this is fine so long as you don't try to generalise from them.
- **Purposive samples**: these are selected for a purpose, for example, TV soap viewers or student drinkers. However, even here, if your primary interest is only in soap viewing or student drinking, you can still construct a reliable sample from these groups, provided that you don't generalise from your findings

about them to make other claims about all TV viewing or general student attitudes.

- **Quota samples**: If – to take the example of our student project on student drinkers – you know from your preliminary background research that the population of student drinkers as a whole includes 70 per cent who drink primarily beer, and 30 per cent who primarily drink other kinds of alcohol, then you need to make sure that these proportions are reflected in your sample – assuming that this question is of interest to your project.
- **Haphazard samples**: e.g. every tenth person, as when you stand in a shopping mall and decide to ask every tenth person who comes along to fill in your questionnaire. This may, or may not, be 'representative' of shoppers generally, so cannot be seen as a strictly scientifically chosen sample.
- **Cluster sampling**: as in the TV ratings, which select samples of households according to 'clusters', first of regions, then of towns, then of neighbourhoods, in order to ensure that the whole country is included. (See Wimmer and Dominick, Chapter 14, for a full explanation of how this is done.)
- **Convenience sample**: again a common choice for student projects. You simply ask the people who are handiest to you (such as all the people living in your hall of residence or dorm) to fill in your questionnaire. This is acceptable for an academic exercise, so long as you don't attempt to generalise to a larger population. That said, it can be possible to construct a representative sample from people who are 'convenient', if you know exactly what you want (research question again!). For example, when Davies et al. constructed their sample of 1,332 6–13-year-olds in schools in England and Wales for their BBC study (*Dear BBC*), they had to rely on 'convenience' in the sense that they approached schools through people who were known to them and who they thought were likely to be receptive. The sample of schools was also designed to be reasonably (although not totally) representative of different types of state school: urban/rural; primary/secondary; inner-city/outer-city; London/ non-London. When we compared our demographic breakdown (gender; age; socio-economic status as measured by special needs status in the schools; media consumption and ownership) we found that our breakdown very closely matched a

similar breakdown of a similar sized sample in a study that *had* been scientifically selected: this was a study carried out by Sonia Livingstone and Moira Bovill at the LSE and published in 1999:*Children, Young People and the Changing Media Environment.* Comparing our sample to theirs was a helpful validity check.

- **Case study:** This is where you focus on just one or two examples of your focus of interest. For instance, if you were studying advertising aimed at young girls, you might choose just one product – shampoo or skin-care cream – and carry out an analysis only on advertising for that product. In the case of research with people, you could choose just one household and study its use of cosmetics and toiletries. An undergraduate student of Máire Messenger Davies at Ulster did a case study of the ads for the Diesel fashion group for her BA dissertation project. She constructed her sample from a time period of two years and chose three different campaigns to look at in detail. She also got some consumer response through a questionnaire with a convenience sample of young people (male and female) in their twenties. This single-case approach allows you to be much more detailed in what you find out. If you are going to focus on particular households, or small groups, this has similarities to ethnographic research carried out by anthropologists in that you may become closely involved in the household yourself while you conduct your survey. We are not giving detailed information about ethnographic methods in this book, although the general principles we recommend about having a proper research question and about general research design and practice apply to all studies with human subjects. We do recommend that if you are conducting qualitative research with human beings, a good ethnographic methods handbook, such as David Machin's *Ethnographic Research for Media Studies* (2002) is useful to consult.

Sampling errors

No sample will be perfect. If the errors (imperfections) are random, then it's not a problem (statistical tests allow for this). The problem arises when you get non-random errors, when there is a pattern of bias in your sample – for instance, you deliberately only talk to young women who wear a particular kind of outfit, when your focus is on young women's attitudes to fashion generally; or young men who support a particular football team, when your focus is on young men's attitudes to football generally.

How do you select a sample?

At the risk of tediously repeating ourselves, we must emphasise again that your choice of sample initially depends on your research question. So once again, it is really important to be clear about **what** you want to know and **why**, and to bear in mind the following **practical** point:

> **Choose a question that can be relatively easily answered *with the resources to hand*, i.e. with a student population, or (in the case of media material) with media archives that can be found in your university or local library, or online**.

If, to take our example above, you want to look at an advertising campaign aimed at young girls, bear in mind the possible difficulty of getting people under eighteen to answer a questionnaire. Ethical issues arise when you are carrying out research with children and teenagers, so you may want to confine your sample to, say, first year undergraduate females. These will be legal adults, but still teenagers (aged 18–19) and likely to be representative of some of the demographics of advertising aimed at young women.

In terms of getting access to advertising material, remember you may not be able to get hold of all the components of the campaign, especially if it's been running for years. Print material is a lot easier to find and study (e.g. it's possible to photocopy it) than television material, so you may decide to stick to ads in magazines and again, just one magazine is easier to sample than several.

Sampling film and television

Because of the relative ease of access, media students often end up doing research on newspapers and magazines rather than film and television. This is a pity, and if you think that you would like to study film and television as part of your research project, start thinking very early on about where you are going to find the material, and tailor your research question accordingly. For instance, getting hold of copies of recent film releases will be difficult because they have not yet been released on DVD or video for the domestic market. Looking at all of 'Hollywood cinema' as one undergraduate announced he was going to do as his dissertation project is completely impossible. It is easier to do an analysis of, say, all adventure film releases in a single week two years ago (which are likely to be available on DVD), or a close comparison of two contrasting single films, or an analysis of one or two evenings' TV output on *one* channel, than to try to survey the whole output of a particular director, or all of 'television advertising'.

Being this selective about your material means, in turn, that your research question has to be very specific (and all the better for it), for instance:

> **'What is the incidence and type of product placements in one week's movie releases, (*in a year from which these releases are available on DVD*); and is there a significant difference in product placements between genres (e.g. action adventure versus romantic comedy)?'**[2]

Sampling television

With television, you can do what we did with a study we conducted for the Broadcasting Standards Commission about the use of children in adult programmes, and whether children were able to consent to the ways in which they were shown on TV (Davies and Mosdell, *Consenting Children?* 2001). We wanted to get a sense of:

> **how often children are used in adult programming on television, in what genres and for what purposes**.

We chose two days in October 2000 and arranged to videotape four terrestrial channels from 6 am until 6 pm on both days. This was still a lot of material to review, but because our question was very specific – the incidence of children in different types of programming – it was

---

[2] For an interesting analysis of product placement in movies, see Toby Miller, Nitin Govil, John McMurria and Richard Maxwell and Ting Wang *Global Hollywood 2* (London: BFI Publishing, 2005), especially Chapter 5, 'Getting the Audience'.

relatively easy to answer. The results, with a brief interpretation of them, are shown below:

Analysis of children in adult TV programming (from Davies and Mosdell, 2001)

- In an analysis of 32 hours of daytime programming on BBC1, ITV, Channel 4 and Channel 5, nearly 13 per cent of material was either aimed at or featured children.
- Most images of children were in adult material: 60 per cent in advertisements; 20 per cent in news broadcasting; 15 per cent in children's programming; and 5 per cent in all other kinds of shows.
- Children's representation had three main characteristics:
  (i)   Passivity – children did not speak, and were not interviewed.
  (ii) Entertainment value – children were 'cute' or 'funny'.
  (iii) Appeals to emotionalism – children were used to evoke sympathy.

Because our sample included both public service (BBC) and commercial channels; because it included all time-periods throughout the day; because it included every type of daytime genre; and because it included both a weekday and a weekend day, we felt confident that this was a *representative sample* of terrestrial daytime programming in general and that the above conclusions were likely to apply to another similar sample of daytime programming.

Sample size
The most frequent question is. 'How many do I need?'

With a large-scale, socially representative sample, where you want to draw conclusions about the population generally, there needs to be at least 100 people in every demographic group. For students, finding such a large group may be difficult if not impossible. As we've said, depending on your research question, your sample should not have to be subdivided into so many groups that any particular subgroup is smaller than five. Statistical tests such as the **chi-square** (see Chapter 10, page 150) become unreliable when numbers in each subgroup are less than this. So again, make your original research question relevant to at the most two or three subgroups (male/female; UK/non-UK students; older/younger) and don't try to analyse more than this.

Beware percentages

The other point to bear in mind is that you will want to translate your numbers into percentages. Percentages become extremely misleading when they are based on small numbers: 10 per cent of a sample of ten people is only one person. You cannot generalise from this. Ten per cent of 100 people is ten people and this is a slightly more reliable number to draw conclusions from, But 10 per cent of 200 people is even better.

Figure 4.1 shows an example of a cross-tabulation in which suchsubdivisions have occurred. This comes from our study of theatre-goers at the West Yorkshire Playhouse in 2001 and shows the proportions of males and females who came from different loca-

Home Base * Sex Crosstabulation

			Sex		Total
			Male	Female	
Home Base	Leeds/Bradford	Count	130	214	344
		% within Home Base	37.8%	62.2%	100.0%
		% within Sex	37.0%	36.4%	36.6%
		% of Total	13.8%	22.8%	36.6%
	Yorkshire Other	Count	120	241	361
		% within Home Base	33.2%	66.8%	100.0%
		% within Sex	34.2%	41.0%	38.4%
		% of Total	12.8%	25.7%	38.4%
	UK Other	Count	98	126	224
		% within Home Base	43.8%	56.3%	100.0%
		% within Sex	27.9%	21.4%	23.9%
		% of Total	10.4%	13.4%	23.9%
	Outside UK	Count	3	7	10
		% within Home Base	30.0%	70.0%	100.0%
		% within Sex	.9%	1.2%	1.1%
		% of Total	.3%	.7%	1.1%
Total		Count	351	588	939
		% within Home Base	37.4%	62.6%	100.0%
		% within Sex	100.0%	100.0%	100.0%
		% of Total	37.4%	62.6%	100.0%

tions: the **variables** entered in the crosstab analysis were 'sex' (in the columns going down) crossed with 'home base' (in the rows going across). As you can see, with such a large sample (939 people) only one of the cells had fewer than five in it. (Can you find it and identify what kind of people these were?) Most of the cells had at least 100 people in each. This made the statistical analysis of the data very reliable.

So the answer to 'How many'? is 'As many as possible within the parameters of your research question'. For instance, adding more people overall to the crosstab above wouldn't have made much difference to the final statistical analysis. However, if we could have found a few more people in the 'outside UK' category, that would have given us more useful comparisons between British and non-British theatre-goers.

For a small-scale student project we suggest you need at least sixty in your questionnaire sample to get anything significant. If you are working in groups of five and you manage to get twenty each, this makes the task for each individual less arduous and will give you a sample of 100. The more data you have, the better chance you have of getting significant results.

CHAPTER 5

The Practicalities

This chapter aims to identify and anticipate some of the possible – and sometimes very real – problems that you may encounter 'in the field'.

Even the most well-funded research will have practical limitations – budget, time, personnel, etc. – and planning the most efficient use of these resources is essential in getting the most from the data that you eventually collect.

Most of this may seem like common sense but it's surprising how many 'Doh' moments we've had as researchers, and how many others have been related to us by students.

Personnel

Your human resources are just as important as any other. When working in groups, in real-world research teams as in student groups, each individual needs to have a clear understanding of the aims of the project and where the work is going at any given time.

We have always found it useful for each group to have a 'minute-taker' – someone who records the group's thoughts from the first brain-storming session through to the end of the project, and who can circulate these to the other members. These notes serve to keep everyone on track and can also be valuable in developing, refining and eventually writing the project report.

Other specific roles can be allocated to other members. Perhaps someone is particularly adept at phrasing questions for the research instrument; someone else may have a flair for designing a questionnaire layout; someone else may relish the task of inputting data (a mind-numbing distraction or a Zen-like state of meditation, depending on your point of view). How you allocate these roles depends on the individuals that make up your particular team; there will inevitably be disagreements and sometimes heated discussion but, as the saying goes, that's life. It can also be constructive for the project as a whole for everyone to feel able to make a contribution to any of the various stages and to debate these ideas with colleagues. In real-world research you will often have to work with people with whom you may not personally agree or even like very much, but it is an important skill to be able to work professionally within a group, whatever the task. Functioning effectively as a team dramatically reduces workload and tension, and increases everyone's involvement in and satisfaction with the project.

Advance planning

Know your audience

Having selected a sample, you need to know where and when they will be available to complete your questionnaire. One of the (many) criticisms about conducting questionnaire-based research is the use of convenience sampling, even though the sample may have been perfectly designed back in the office or classroom. If you intend to sample members of the public, think about the bias that you will introduce if you hand out questionnaires only in a town centre on a weekday lunchtime.

One of the examples that we use in teaching this module comes from the West Yorkshire Playhouse data. We gave out questionnaires over three days, and over different performance times during those days. One simple finding was that the vast majority of the Friday matinee performance was aged over sixty-five. Why might that be? Because other age groups were at work? Because there was a particular, age-related discount on those days? Because that particular age demographic felt less comfortable about going out in the evenings?

A neat example comes from (yet another) student project about alcohol consumption in student union bars. Think about how time of day might affect this, not just in terms of who might be actually capable of filling in a questionnaire, but who the clientele of the bars are at different times of the day. Are people who are questioned at midday likely to give different answers about their weekly alcohol consumption from those questioned at midnight? Are those questioned at midnight on a Friday likely to give different answers from those questioned at midnight on a Monday? Are those questioned at midnight on a Friday likely to give different answers than those questioned at 9 pm on a Friday?

Are those questioned at 2.00 a.m. likely to give any answer at all? (The group in question dealt with this by sampling at different times on different days, and had a lot of fun doing so.)

On a more serious note, if you intend to conduct research any-where other than a public area, those who are 'hosting' your target sample will want to know exactly what you are doing as well. We have had several students conducting research into various airlines that have run into all sorts of difficulties from airport authorities in the cur-rent security climate, although they were very supportive in the end. This can be useful – if you gain the permission and approach the 'hosts' with honesty, they may well come up with suggestions that can aid your project. The project with the West Yorkshire Playhouse was conducted in close partnership with their marketing department, which made a number of suggestions for questions based on their own expertise and experience, which were invaluable to the final work.

Special care has to be taken when working with vulnerable groups – in particular children. These themes are addressed in Chapter 9. See also the section on ethics below, pp. 75–6.

Know your venue

We decided, and were given permission, to hand out questionnaires at the West Yorkshire Playhouse.

Where is the West Yorkshire Playhouse?

Traffic will be late, roads will be jammed, offices will be down a tiny side street that is invisible to all but those who work there and that are, in reality, in a completely different area/city/continent from the main reception building.

Make sure you know where you are going; how to get there; how long it will take (plus additional times for unexpected 'adventures').

Thinking about these things in advance will significantly reduce stress.

Check your instruments

Make sure you have a sufficient number of questionnaires printed or photocopied and bring more than you think you might need.

If you are planning to photocopy questionnaires at the venue, make sure you know where these facilities are (and that they are working).

Bring pencils. Lots and lots of pencils. Far more than you think you will need. Unless you are administering the questionnaire face-to-face, pencils will get lost behind chairs or wander off on their own.

Remember to number the questionnaires when they have been completed. This will not only make data entry easier (ensuring that you don't enter the same data set twice) but will also allow you to separate out which questionnaires were given out and where. This can also be useful when you come to analyse the data. Mistakes may be made during data entry, but if the questionnaire is numbered, it's easy to go back and check.

Ethical considerations

Whenever you are doing research with people you need to consider the ethics of the project. This involves being polite and courteous, but also not deliberately misleading people in any way, and keeping their responses confidential.

As we have suggested in Chapter 6, it's always useful to have some sort of introduction at the beginning of your questionnaire that sets out the ground rules. This should include a statement about the nature of the project both as a way of getting your respondents into the right frame of mind to think about the topic, and also as reassurance that the research is for academic purposes and not market research or collection of personal information. Try not to give too much away here though – it's equally important that you don't introduce bias by detailing your hypotheses, and perhaps thereby subconsciously influencing possible responses.

It is also very important to state that it is an academic project. There are no right or wrong answers and you want people to respond honestly, but the information will not be used for any other purpose (e.g. marketing information). All information is also confidential. You will not usually ask people their names or contact details, but if you do – perhaps as a way of recruiting people for follow-up focus groups – it's important to reassure them that this information will not be given to a third party.

Finally, many universities have standards of ethics that apply to all kinds of research. These are more obvious if you are thinking about a project that involves vulnerable groups such as children; some of these concerns are set out in Chapter 9. However, collecting personal information from members of the public may also raise ethical and practical issues. It's worth discussing these with a lecturer but, since the primary focus of this book is to illustrate these methods as an exercise, it may be safer to stick with conducting your research on classmates and other students.

The seven P's

We have found the following checklist very useful in preparing and conducting field research.

Personnel

Make sure everyone in the team has a role but also has a clear understanding of everyone else's role, and of the project direction as a whole.

Piloting

Make sure you test your questionnaire for presentation, administration and wording. Run a simple **pilot** on a few classmates and check the results. Chapter 8 discusses the value of piloting in more detail.

Pencils

You can never have too many.

Photocopying

Make sure you have sufficient copies of the questionnaire, and then add some more. If you intend to get the instrument copied at the location where you intend to do the research, make sure you have confirmed access and financial details for copying.

Plan B

Be prepared for things to go wrong. It's always worth trying to anticipate any potential hiccups in the entire research process and thinking of alternative solutions. Again, the process of piloting will inform your thinking here.

Planning

Thinking carefully about the practical administration of the questionnaire will reduce stress considerably.

Pholders

OK, so we cheated a bit there. Maintaining good records and carefully storing completed data are crucial though, and having a filing and storage system that all group members understand will avoid problems when you come to look at the data.

The following chapters discuss instrument design in more detail but bear these practicalities in mind all the way through the project.

CHAPTER 6

Instrument Design: The Questionnaire

In this chapter, we discuss the main research instrument used in quantitative research methods: **the questionnaire**, used for surveys with members of the public. We address this topic from a number of points of view, bearing in mind: the practicalities of administration (in the case of questionnaires, often in a public place); the diversity of the sample, especially if you are dealing with a representative sample of people with different interest, intelligence and education levels; the internal validity (does the instrument address the questions you are interested in?); and the clarity of subsequent analysis, whether quantitative or qualitative.

Questionnaire design

A questionnaire is one of the simplest and quickest ways of getting information from large numbers of people and, with modern versions of statistical software, it can be a very easy instrument both to design and analyse. However, the people you ask to answer it may not find it easy at all – so careful design is very important in order to get the clearest answers to your questions.

In general, simple questionnaires of the kind used in student projects (and, we believe, simplicity is also a virtue of professional questionnaire design) is likely to have just two main sections (as we said in Chapter 3):

1. **A demographic section** – in which respondents give information about themselves relevant to your project, including the standard demographic information about age and gender.
2. **An information/attitude section** – in this section people answer the questions you are interested in as part of your research project.

In the case of media research, a third section may be desirable, asking about people's media consumption, habits and tastes. For instance, you may have a hunch (hypothesis) that people who read the tabloid press might be more inclined to be sympathetic to the royal family than people who read broadsheet newspapers. So you may want to include a section on what newspapers people read and how often, and then check whether tabloid readers have more positive answers to questions about royalty – a project that an undergraduate group of students in a BA module we taught wanted to carry out. People's tastes in film, television, books and music may also be **correlated** (see Chapter 10) with social class or other demographic characteristics or social attitudes. So, again, *depending on your research question*, information about people's general media consumption may be useful.

Relating the research question to question design

Once again, to emphasise the importance of having a clear research question and how this will helpfully influence your instrument design, we draw on an example from our own research. In our West Yorkshire Playhouse study, in which we were interested in the relationship between people's attitudes to popular culture (such as television watching) and 'high' culture (such as theatre-going) we asked for information about both, as follows:

Every day I watch TV for	5 or more hours	3–4 hours	1–2 hours	1 hour or less	Never

and

I go to the theatre	6–12 times a year	2–5 times a year	Once a year	Less than once a year	Never

Among the 903 theatre-goers who answered these questions, we found a **significant correlation** (see Chapter 10) between amount of television watching and regular theatre-going, with the highest concentrations of answers coming in the 1–2 hours TV group (188 people, 48.5 per cent of the television viewers) who also went to the theatre 6–12 times a year. There was also a high concentration of people in the 3–4 hours a day TV group who went to the theatre 2–5 times a year (102 people, 46.2 per cent of this group of TV viewers). There was no relationship at all between heavy TV viewing and *never* going to the theatre, which was what some people might expect if they believe that watching TV is lowbrow and going to the theatre is more intellectually highbrow. Our focus group discussions supported these question-naire findings: the people who volunteered for the groups, some very passionate theatre-goers, were also very knowledgeable and enthusias-tic about television. Not surprisingly, considering the star of the play (Patrick Stewart), some of these people were also passionate *Star Trek* fans – and again, very far from the geeky, 'Trekkie' stereotype. This kind of research is valuable in '**falsifying**' (see Chapter 1) popular, and academic, assumptions about class-related cultural habits.

Designing your questions

Questionnaires are a very quick way of gathering a lot of data, but the quality of those data depends a great deal on:

- the clarity with which you have formulated your research question;
- the extent to which the questions in your questionnaire are related to the research question;
- the wording of the questions and their comprehensibility to the people answering;
- the extent to which you don't prompt desired answers in your respondents by asking leading questions.

Avoiding leading questions

Questions should not lead your respondents in the direction you hope they will go. For instance, if we had asked our West Yorkshire res-pondents: 'Television watching is more lower-class than going to the theatre', we would have pointed them towards one of the possible desired answers underlying our research question; some people might have been tempted to circle the 'agree' or 'strongly agree' boxes, be-cause they know that many academic researchers disapprove of tele-vision, and might have thought that this was the answer we wanted. Asking a behavioural question about what people *did*, whether going to the theatre or watching television, was more revealing. Even though their answers were only *estimates* of their habits and perhaps not entirely accurate, there was still a positive relationship between both sets of estimates: they *saw themselves* as both regular TV viewers and regular theatre-goers without any apparent inconsistency.

Closed and open-ended questions

As we've said, questions can be *closed* or *open-ended*. For ease of coding, the most common form is closed-ended, in which a question is posed and a list of possible answers is provided (**multiple-choice**). Open-ended questions allow the respondents to answer in as much detail as they wish, and good questionnaires, as we've pointed out, include opportunities for people to do both.

If your target audience is likely to be very multicultural, it can be problematic to provide an exhaustive list of possible responses, particularly in the cases of nationality or religion. In such cases, it may be better to allow respondents to write in their answers and then post-code these once the data have been collected.

Questionnaire structure

The demographics section – information about the people themselves and their characteristics – usually appears first on the questionnaire. These are straightforward questions to answer and may put your respondents at ease. However, again, don't put too many of these types of questions in – only use those relevant to your research question. You don't want the questionnaire to appear pointless or boring (or indeed, impertinent, if you ask too many personal questions). If you do feel it is necessary to include several demographic questions, you can always have some at the beginning (as a 'warm-up' to the questionnaire) and the rest at the end.

Giving 'grouped' options for variables such as age (e.g. age 25–30; 31–35; 36–40) and income (e.g. under £10,000; £11,000–15,000, and so on) is standard practice. Here's an example from our West Yorkshire Playhouse questionnaire:

A. ABOUT YOU

Please **circle** the appropriate category, e.g. if you are 28 years old, circle 26–35:

Age (years)	0–10	11–16	17–25	26–35	36–45	46–55	56–65	65+

Annual household income	Below £10,000	£10,000– £20,000	£21,000– £35,000	£36,000– £50,000	£51,000– £70,000	£71,000– £90,000	Above £91,000

We also give an example from a student questionnaire about attitudes to alcohol, which – again as determined by the research question – does not include age-groups under eighteen because the question is about drinking habits. Asking under-eighteens (who quite clearly do drink alcohol sometimes) would not be advisable for ethical and practical reasons in a student project:

2. What is your age group?

☐ 18–25   ☐ 26–35   ☐ 36–45   ☐ 46+

Getting to the point of your research

The most important section will be where you directly address the research topic that you are investigating. Here you are more likely to use a mixture of closed-ended, multiple-choice questions and those that try to tap into the respondents' feelings and attitudes towards the topic.

Below, we use an example from a student project on drinking habits and attitudes to illustrate the basic principles of questionnaire design. We will also use data from student projects to illustrate our later chapters about data analysis and interpretation. We stress that these are examples for teaching and exercise purposes: they are a *how to* illustration, not a model to follow in real-world research (although in fact, this project on drinking is not a bad piece of research, even from a professional point of view). The students' original questionnaire is printed in bold type; our comments are in normal type.

Questionnaire on drinking habits

In the case used here, the students have not headlined their questionnaire 'drinking habits'. Sometimes such a headline can be off-putting to respondents, especially if it's a sensitive topic. However, as must be done with all questionnaires, the students do identify themselves as being from Cardiff University and explain why they are doing the research (for a student project); they also promise confidentiality. You will note that there is no space on the questionnaire for the name of the person answering. If you *do* ask for the person's name, you *must* keep it confidential. All questionnaires, once completed, must be numbered. When you enter the data into the SPSS program, the number on the questionnaire MUST correspond to the number in the data set, i.e. the person who filled in questionnaire No. 1 should be the first person whose data you enter in SPSS 'data view' (see Chapter 10). The reason for this should be obvious: if you need to check the accuracy of your SPSS data, or if there are qualitative comments on the questionnaire of person No. 1 (or 51, or 151) which need to be matched to the quantitative responses, we need to be able to put our hands quickly on questionnaire No. 1 (or 51, or 151). Accurate numbering of all completed questionnaires is one of the most essential jobs in carrying out surveys. We give an example below from our West Yorkshire data set of the first two people who answered our questionnaire.

S	Performance attended	Age	Sex	Ethnicity	Income	Education	Homebase
1.	Thursday Matinee (13/09/01)	65+	Female	White	99.00	Postgraduate	UK Other
2.	Thursday Matinee (13/09/01)	65+	Female	White	£10–20k	HE	Leeds/ Bradford

As we can see, S (Subject) No. 1 attended the Thursday matinee performance, was in the 65+ age group, was female, white, didn't give her income, was educated to postgraduate level and came from the UK outside Yorkshire. The topics in bold across the top of the columns are the first seven **variables** in our West Yorkshire survey, and the answers that these women gave are the **values** (levels) associated with these variables. All had been numerically coded. 'Female' had been coded 2, with 'male' 1; Postgrad had been coded '6' out of six levels of education; 'UK other' had been coded 3 (one of four different categories for where people lived). If we wanted to know more about subject No. 1, and what her comments were in the 'other' section, or if she'd volunteered for a focus group, we would go to the hard copy of the questionnaire labelled '1'. This seems so eminently common sense that it would seem not worth saying; however, we have bitter experience of coming across unnumbered questionnaires and not being able to identify the data associated with them in our data sets. Sitting down with a cup of tea and one of your pencils (see Chapter 5) and numbering your questionnaires as soon as you've collected them, then putting them in a folder labelled 'Thursday Matinee, Nos. 1–150' can save hours of grief.

Cardiff student questionnaire example:

Disclaimer: **We are students at Cardiff University and are undertaking a study for our MA programme and would be very grateful for your comments. Your responses are confidential and strictly for research purposes only.**

1. What is your gender?

☐ **Male**   ☐ **Female**

2. What is your age group?

☐ **18–25**   ☐ **26–35**   ☐ **36–45**   ☐ **46+**

3. What is your employment status? (Please select more than one if necessary)

☐ **Unemployed**

☐ **Self-employed**

☐ **Full-time employment**

☐ **Part-time employment**

☐ **Student**

☐ **Other** .... **(please specify)**

☐ **Retired**

The demographic section ends here, and the next section – getting to the point of the research, with fourteen questions about drinking habits and attitudes to them – starts very helpfully with some explanations of what 'a unit' means when applied to alcoholic drinks:

If a pint of lager is 2 units; a glass of wine is 1 unit; a single measure of a spirit is 1 unit and the average cocktail is 3 units:

4. **On average how many units of alcohol do you consume in the average week?**

   ☐ **None** ☐ **1–10** ☐ **11–20** ☐ **21–30** ☐ **31–40**
   ☐ **40+**

5. **How many times on average would you say you consumed alcohol?**

   ☐ **None**
   ☐ **Once/twice a week**
   ☐ **Three/four times a week**
   ☐ **Every other day**
   ☐ **Everyday**

6. **Where do you usually consume alcohol? (Please choose up to three answers and rank answers 1–3, with 1 being most often and 3 being the third most likely)**

   ☐ **At home** ☐ **Pub** ☐ **Restaurant**
   ☐ **Bar** ☐ **Club** ☐ **Other (please specify)**

   This is an example of 'multiple responses' – in other words, people are being given the option of ticking more than one box. There is a way of dealing with this when it comes to analysing the data which we explain in Appendix 2 ('Multiple-responses').

7. **Do you drink in order to get drunk?**

   ☐ **Yes** ☐ **Occasionally** ☐ **Don't know**

8. **Do you have concerns for your health if you drink regularly?**

   ☐ **Yes** ☐ **Sometimes** ☐ **No** ☐ **Don't know**

9. **For the purposes of this questionnaire we are using *Alcohol Concern*'s definition of binge drinking: 'Drinking sufficient alcohol to reach a state of intoxication in the course of one drinking session.' To what extent do you agree?**

☐ **Strongly agree**

☐ **Agree**

☐ **Somewhat agree**

☐ **Neither agree nor disagree**

☐ **Somewhat disagree**

☐ **Disagree**

☐ **Strongly disagree**

Again, these students have helpfully found an official definition of the term 'binge drinking' – a term widely used but not often defined – in order to help their respondents answer the question.

You will notice that they are using a seven-point scale for this first question – sometimes used, but less often than the five-point scale for reasons which you may spot yourself. For instance, if you have to decide between 'agree' and 'somewhat agree' how do you do this? It's simpler for people (especially those in a hurry) to distinguish between 'strong feeling' and just 'feeling'. If you subdivide your answers by seven rather than five, you will also get fewer subjects in each category and, as we pointed out in Chapter 4, the smaller the subgroups in your sample, the less reliable your findings will be.

From now on, the students are using a five-point scale, and they are also varying the wording of their questions, as with questions 11, 14 and 17. This is a good idea to stop people answering routinely; if the format of the question is always the same, the temptation to make the format of the answer the same is greater.

10. **'I need to consume alcohol on a regular basis just to have a good time.' To what extent do you agree?**

☐ **Strongly agree**

☐ **Agree**

☐ Neither agree nor disagree

☐ Disagree

☐ Strongly disagree

11. **When drinking in groups, would you say that you were more likely drink in 'rounds' or buy your own drinks individually?**

☐ Drink in rounds   ☐ Buy drinks individually

☐ It varies   ☐ Don't know

12. **'It has been suggested that drinking in rounds leads to binge drinking.' To what extent do you agree?**

☐ Strongly agree

☐ Agree

☐ Neither agree nor disagree

☐ Disagree

☐ Strongly disagree

13. **'When I see an advertisement for an alcoholic product, I feel driven to purchase it.' To what extent do you agree?**

☐ Strongly agree

☐ Agree

☐ Neither agree nor disagree

☐ Disagree

☐ Strongly disagree

14. **Do you think that the Government is right to introduce legislation where drinking establishments have 24-hour licences?**

☐ Yes   ☐ To an extent   ☐ No   ☐ Don't know

15. **'The 24-hour licensing for the sale of alcohol will cut down on anti-social behaviour.' To what extent do you agree?**

☐ Strongly agree

☐ Agree

☐ Neither agree nor disagree

☐ Disagree

☐ Strongly disagree

16. **'The Government is going to introduce a policy to ban the selling of alcohol on public transport, i.e. aeroplanes and trains.' To what extent do you believe this will be successful in restraining binge drinking culture?**

☐ Strongly agree

☐ Agree

☐ Neither agree nor disagree

☐ Disagree

☐ Strongly disagree

The wording of this question is a little complicated. People are being asked to what extent they believe 'this', but it's not clear at first glance what 'this' refers to. Is it aeroplanes and trains? The Government? Or is it in fact the policy? It is in fact the policy, so simplifying the question might have been wiser, e.g.:

'Banning the sale of alcohol on public transport will reduce binge drinking.'

17. **Do you think that the consumption of alcohol can be connected to antisocial behaviour?**

☐ Yes   ☐ Indirectly linked   ☐ No   ☐ Don't know

This could be seen as an example of a 'leading question'. Obviously, it's an example of the good practice of varying wording, but it might have been better to make it a Likert scale statement:

'The consumption of alcohol is directly connected to antisocial behaviour.'

Or it could have been worded even more precisely to avoid what are sometimes called 'hidden contingencies'. That is, a person answering the questionnaire might have different definitions of 'antisocial' than the researchers. Again, being specific is the better way:

'Drinking alcohol makes people aggressive.'

Or

'Drinking alcohol contributes to rowdy behaviour in the street.'

18. Do you have any other comments?

. . . .

. . . .

. . . .

~ THANK YOU FOR COMPLETING THIS QUESTIONNAIRE ~

Presentation

Even if you are administering the questionnaire in person, the design and layout reflect your status as a researcher. Spelling mistakes and sloppy layout will not make your respondents feel confident in your abilities, so do your best to make the presentation as professional as possible. It's also very important to be as simple as possible. Even if you are giving a questionnaire to a group of people who pride themselves on being intellectuals, clarity and an absence of ambiguity are essential in good questionnaire design: the simpler and clearer the language, the better.

Introduction

It is a good idea to have some sort of brief introduction at the top of the first page. This should include the name of the institution you are working for and a brief outline of the project. It is very important that you do not give too much information away here though. As we've said, telling respondents all about your hypotheses before they answer the questions will inevitably influence their answers and bias your data. You can also use this space to state the purposes of the data (e.g. research for your undergraduate project) and to emphasise the facts that:

- Respondents do not have to answer any questions that they feel uncomfortable with (some people do not like stating their age or salary, for example).
- The data will not be used for any other purpose. This is especially relevant if you have asked them to give contact details (for example, for follow-up focus groups or telephone interviews). If this is the case, you should also stress that they will remain anonymous in any reports that you prepare.
- It is also worth stating that there are no right or wrong answers – this is particularly the case with younger children. Respondents should be encouraged to be as honest and open as possible in their answers.

How long?

The most frequent question we have from our students is 'How long should the questionnaire be?' Unfortunately, there is no simple answer. Whether singly or as a research team, you should consider some of the following issues that will have a bearing on the number of questions that you can reasonably ask:

- What are the most important demographic questions?
  There is no point in including questions simply because they pad out the questionnaire or because they might have some vague bearing on your research question.

- What are the most important research questions?
  Remember you are likely to get only one shot at collecting your data so try to ensure that you cover all of the areas you are interested in. The ways in which these questions are structured is vital, so try to think creatively and bear in mind the comments we made

about the student questionnaire and its wording, above. Remember the value of piloting the first draft (see Chapter 8).

- Who will be answering your questionnaire?
  Someone who is approached in their lunch-break or during a shopping trip will not be very likely to answer a questionnaire that looks as thick as a telephone directory and that takes more than a couple of minutes to complete. Someone who is sent the questionnaire via e-mail or post, or who deliberately visits a website to answer it, is likely to have a bit more time. The length of the questionnaire is crucial in determining your *response rate* (the number of people who complete the instrument) and a common cause of a low response rate is an over-long questionnaire that looks time-consuming or that becomes so tedious that people don't finish it. This will undermine **internal validity**. It will also distort your sample, which will end up consisting only of very patient or under-employed people, and this undermines **external validity**. Again, piloting will help here.

- How will you administer the questionnaire?
  Questionnaires that you hand out or leave for respondents to complete themselves must not look intimidating. If you are administering the questionnaire yourselves (face to face with the respondent or via the telephone), it is common courtesy to give the respondent some indication of how long it will take. You will know this, of course, from having piloted your questionnaire first.

Question structure

The way in which you ask your questions will have great bearing on the quality and validity of the data that you collect. It is important to spend time considering the detail of the wording and again, this is where **piloting**, even if only on one other person, is essential. In our class workshops, we always have some form of exercise in which students either work in pairs, first answering and then critiquing each other's research instruments, or in groups, and the groups swap their draft instruments with each other. This way, a group can get at least five responses to their questionnaire, and also some useful criticisms of it from their peers.

Standard demographics

These will include some or all of the following: age; gender; income; nationality; ethnicity; education; religion; number of children (and ages); home base. Other demographic information (for instance, in the case of the drinking project above) could include employment or student status.

Considerations of coding

These, and your intended analyses based on coding, will influence the design of the responses to demographic questions, for example, as we've said, using grouped categories such as a span of a few years for age (e.g. Under 15; 16–20; 21–25, etc.). Multiple-choice questions also facilitate ease of coding, as does the standard five-point Likert scale.

Research questions

Most questionnaires include questions which relate to attitudes (approval/disapproval; likes/dislikes; agree/disagree, and so on) or frequencies of behaviour (for example, of television viewing or of consumption of a particular product). Social science and humanities students and researchers are particularly interested in people's opinions and tastes. As we explained in Chapter 3, the most common way to get at people's attitudes is through the Likert five-point scale, asking people to express levels of agreement or disagreement with a statement.

Some do's and don'ts

The wording of the statement is often crucial here.

- Don't make statements that appear to have a very obvious answer.
- Don't make statements requiring extremely complicated judgements.
- Do make statements that are thought-provoking to try to elicit a range of responses.
- Do try to avoid offending your respondents' sensitivities.
- Do think carefully about who will be answering your questions and the amount of knowledge that they are likely to have about

particular topics. This will avoid eliciting the 'don't know/neutral' response too often.

- Do provide enough space for the respondents to elaborate or specify. Such responses can later be post-coded.

Neutral/don't know/undecided

The mid-point on a Likert scale may attract people who like to 'sit on the fence'. This can be avoided by using a four-point scale in which the respondent is 'forced' to express some degree of, for example, agreement or disagreement. However, a high number of neutral responses may actually be revealing; they may reflect a problem with the wording of your question (which you will pick up and amend at the piloting stage) or the fact that your sample, or a particular subgroup of your sample, really do feel neutral about that issue. This is a finding. Hence, we recommend that you play safe with the five-point scale and are very precise about your wording.

Checking internal validity

If you are concerned about the possibility of respondents answering in a haphazard way, then it is sometimes useful to have another question aimed at the same topic but that is phrased differently, perhaps even with the scales reversed. This will allow you to check respondents' consistency. For example, in the drinking questionnaire: 'I need to drink alcohol in order to have a good time' you could include another question later in the questionnaire: 'You can have a really successful party without alcohol', plus the 'agree/disagree' scale. A person who strongly agreed with the first question is likely to strongly disagree with the second. There will be a **negative correlation** between the two answers.

Response set

Reversing the scales of questions will also help to prevent respondents developing a pattern of responses, for example, always ticking 'strongly agree', known as 'response set'. The above example about drinking shows how you get round this: a social drinker will have to tick 'disagree' on the second question.

Qualitative data

Although much of the data from a questionnaire will be considered as quantitative, as we've said, you can often benefit from adding space at the end of the questionnaire to allow respondents to add their own comments. Many of these will not relate directly to your topic; some may be downright insulting (for instance, there will always be a few members of the public who know much better than you do how to design a questionnaire). But there may well be some valuable nuggets that draw attention to aspects of the topic that you may not have considered before.

A brief revision of key terms

We described how to code a very simple 'baby questionnaire', with only five questions, in Chapter 3. Here we revisit these terms to remind you that, now you've designed a more extensive and professional-looking questionnaire, these are the tasks that await you.

Coding

Before you can begin the task of analysing your data you need to put it in a form that the computer software can deal with. Coding is assigning numbers to your answers. REMEMBER THE DATA TYPES THAT YOU HAVE SEEN BEFORE: nominal; ordinal; interval/ scale (see Chapter 3). Also, have another look at the example of the first two lines from the West Yorkshire data set and see how you could adapt them for coding your own project (p. 83).

Variables

Each aspect that you want to look at is called a **variable**. For example, one variable is likely to be gender and you may decide that a person's gender will have an effect on one of your other variables, such as their attitude to television news or, in the case of the West Yorkshire study, their visits to the theatre. The variables in this study were chosen when we designed our questionnaire because we thought they'd be relevant to our basic question about the cultural habits of theatre-goers. Variable 7, 'home base', for instance, was useful to us in revealing just how far some people were prepared to travel to go to the theatre and

see a favourite actor. Usually, each of the questions on your questionnaire can be considered as a separate variable and so each needs to be
coded before you can do any analysis using SPSS.

Demographic factors are often described as **independent variables**. That is, they are assumed to function 'independently' in such
a way that they *influence* the other factors that you are interested in,
such as people's attitudes to Irish politics, or binge drinking, or
theatre-going. The factors that *are influenced* by these independent
demographic characteristics (age, sex, nationality, etc.) are called
dependent variables, because the influence doesn't work (at least
in research design) the other way round: your attitude to Irish politics
isn't going to influence which sex you are, for example, but your sex
may influence your views on politics.

Independent variables may not always be demographic factors;
in an experimental study, the factor exerting an influence on how
people behave, or perform, can also be something created by the exp-
erimenter.[1] For instance, one dissertation student we worked with was
interested in the difference between tabloid layout and broadsheet
layout of the front pages of newspapers and the possible different
effects this would have on the ways in which readers remembered
the content. She was also interested in online versions of these front
pages. Did the online version influence people's understanding and
recall more than, or differently from, the print version? Did the tabloid version produce different responses from the broadsheet version?
In this case, the **independent variables** were the experimental
conditions that she manipulated: in one condition students saw a
broadsheet version, in the other, a tabloid version. The name of this
variable could be 'page design' or 'layout type'.

Values

The numbers that you assign to each possible answer of the question
are known as the **values** of that variable. If we look at gender, the

---

[1] We have not talked much about experiments here, as experiments are rarely chosen
as a research tool by media and humanities students, and they are not often appropriate for the kinds of questions these students want to ask. But both of us, as trained
psychology graduates, believe strongly in the value of experiments as research tools
for certain kinds of specific research questions, for instance, questions to do with variations in media format.

values of that variable could be 1 to stand for males and 2 to stand for females – it makes no difference which, as these are 'nominal' data. You can use 1, 2, 3, etc. as values for the next variable (for example, age). In the West Yorkshire study, there were eight values for age. When coding, you need to give a value to ALL of the possible answers for EACH question. This will help you enter your data later.

Post-coding

In some circumstances it will not be possible to assign codes before you have looked at the data. This is quite legitimate. For example, if you ask people what their favourite television programme is, it would be impossible to anticipate all of the possible answers in advance. Similarly, sometimes you may want to analyse some of the qualitative data that you get from comment sections – those labelled 'Other' or 'Do you have any further comments?'

Post-coding is the same as pre-coding, but you do it as you go along. Start with your first completed questionnaire and assign '1' to the first instance on the specific question. Each time you come to a new answer simply assign a value to it. For example, if the answer to 'What is your favourite television programme' in the first questionnaire you analyse is 'EastEnders', you code 'EastEnders' as 1; every time you come across this answer, you code it as '1'. If the next questionnaire has 'Blind Date' in answer to this question, this is coded as 2, and every time someone says 'Blind Date', you code it '2'. It's worth noting that the range of favourites in answers to such questions can be very wide, with codings going up to 300 or so – there can be hundreds of different responses in a large sample. This gives an indication of the diversity of people's tastes and is another important, but sometimes neglected, measure of media influence. With this kind of survey, not only do we find out what the most frequently mentioned programmes are (usually the top-rated shows, like 'EastEnders') we also find out the range, variety and distribution of people's tastes – something not mentioned so much in standard competitive league tables, like 'Top Tens'.

Piloting

We can do nothing at all with our design instruments without piloting them first. It is absolutely vital that, before you do any research with members of the public, or with material for a content analysis, you try it out first with a few volunteers in the case of questionnaires, or with some sample texts in the case of content analysis. Piloting enables you to identify any problems with your instruments and procedures (for instance, questions that are hard for people to understand, or coding categories that don't make sense to other coders) in advance of carrying out the investigation proper. Piloting is discussed in Chapter 8, but before we talk about this essential ingredient of all good empirical research, we turn to the question which many media students want to answer: How do you apply quantitative research methods to the analysis of media texts, whether word or image: the technique of **content analysis**?

Test questions: Chapter 6: questionnaire design

1. In the student questionnaire on pages 84–9, can you think of any further information you would have added to the introduction of this questionnaire?
2. You are conducting a project on young people's attitudes to 'celebrity culture'. Construct two Likert-scale statements evaluating these attitudes.
3. Show them to a colleague and amend them, if necessary, according to the following guidelines:

   • Don't give statements that appear to have a very obvious answer.
   • Don't give statements that require extremely complicated judgements.
   • Do make statements that are thought-provoking to try to elicit a range of responses.
   • Do try to avoid offending your respondents' sensitivities.

4. How would you code the following three subjects' characteristics, giving both **variable labels** and their number codings and **value labels** with their number codings?

   S. No. 1: 25-year-old male student, studying BA history, originating from France, parents' occupations doctor and university lecturer.
   S. No. 2: 40-year-old female, occupation transport worker, originating from North London, parents' occupations not given.

CHAPTER 7

Content Analysis

Content analysis is a very common method in media studies. There are many texts that deal with the weightier concepts behind this popular technique, but the aim of this chapter is to give some ideas about how to actually go about conducting a quantitative content analysis.

What is it?

Quantitative content analysis does pretty much what it says – it is a *systematic* and *objective* analysis of any particular text, whether a newspaper article, a book, a television clip or an advert. The quantitative aspect distinguishes this method from other more qualitative techniques. What we are doing here is essentially counting things – how many articles in a given time period; how many instances of a particular word, and so on.

As with other quantitative techniques, objectivity and rigour are vital, but especially so in content analysis to avoid accusations of deliberately creating a technique that will find what you are looking for. The ways in which your sample and your measurements are defined are very important in your methodology section and we aim to deal with these below.

Strictly speaking, content analysis is a quantitative method but it is often confused with other ways of looking at texts. Other ways of analysing texts include more qualitative methods such as visual and discourse analysis. These techniques aim to investigate less systematic (perhaps more subjective) concepts of meaning and association and involve a great deal of attention being paid to each individual text. Quantitative content analysis will allow you to analyse a greater number of examples of a particular type of text by applying the same criteria to each instance.

What it is not

It is very important to realise that content analysis is simply a quantitative description of what the text contains. You cannot make any other inferences from this, and the technique has often been abused in this way. For example, just because 57 per cent of television adverts during a (carefully selected) sample period of children's television programming were for this year's must-have children's toy does not mean that they created a desire in children to purchase it or to pester adults into doing so.

There is absolutely no guarantee that the viewers even watched the advert, never mind suddenly had a desire for the product. Likewise, a comprehensive analysis of the linguistic elements of a newspaper article or book assumes that the piece was actually read in detail, not simply skimmed or ignored completely.

An example we use in teaching this idea is that of television advertising. In the UK there was a visually stunning advert for a particular brand of automobile. The advert clearly cost a great deal of money to produce and the majority of the class could recall having seen it and could describe it in detail. However, not a single person could name the car manufacturer, let alone the specific model that was being advertised.

Technical terms

Before continuing, it is important to become familiar with two key terms.

Unit of analysis

This is your text – where you will find the information you are interested in – and what specific part of the text you will be analysing. For example, if you are interested in looking at newspaper coverage of a particular topic you will need to think about the following:

a) Which newspapers will I look at?
b) How will I create a sample of these newspapers (if a sample is needed)?
c) What specifically will I analyse?
   • Just the articles on the front page or all articles in the newspaper that relate to the topic?
   • Just the headline?
   • Just the images that accompany the text?

- Do I treat the whole article as a single entity or should I break it down into paragraphs or sentences?

Considerations that are specific to different media are dealt with in more detail below.

Units of measurement

These are the things that you are looking for within your unit of analysis and will depend very much on your research questions/hypotheses. If, for example, you are looking at newspaper coverage and consider the whole article to be your unit of analysis, some simple things to look for might be date of the article, word length and how many times a particular theme is mentioned. More details are provided later in this chapter.

Where to start?

As with questionnaire design, the first place to start is with your hypotheses. These will help you work out your *sample, units of analysis* and *units of measurement* so that you can construct a coding sheet that allows you to gather data to support (or refute) your ideas. Think carefully about what it is you want to investigate and where and how you will find the evidence to help you do this.

Another way of looking at this is to think backwards from your 'findings and conclusions' section in a report. What is it *exactly* that you want to say, and what elements of a text will help you investigate and provide evidence for this?

It is especially important to give *operational definitions* of all of the elements of your research questions/hypotheses. This means being very specific about what it is that you are looking for and will guide you in the selection of your sample, and the design of your coding sheet. For example, if your hypothesis is that 'media coverage of topic X is biased', you must be able to give very precise definitions of:

- Media coverage – Newspapers? Television? Magazines? From when?
- Topic X – What particular aspect of the topic?
- Biased – One-sided? Ill-informed? Compared with what?

Sampling

Sampling techniques for content analysis throw up a set of specific issues in addition to those found in other quantitative methods (for example, surveys). These are influenced by two factors:

1. your topic;
2. your unit of analysis (the material).

Census

If you are studying an event or a topic that has a discrete time period and a manageable amount of material, it may be possible to take a *census* – that is, to look at *all* of the occurrences of this material. One example might be a particular billboard advertising campaign that might have just a few different examples.

Event-driven

You may be studying the coverage of a particular event that occurs over a specific time period, for example, a political election. You will need to consider the time-frame of the event in order to decide your sample. Clearly, there will be more coverage as the election approaches and at certain 'peak' times (when the candidates are announced or when a major speech is given). You will need to think carefully about your hypotheses in order to construct a sample that addresses the relevant aspects of this.

To continue with this example, if you are looking at the coverage of a particular political organisation over a year, you will need to take any such 'peaks' into account. You might need to think about how you would analyse the coverage of the key issues and then construct a sample period in which relatively little is happening as a comparison.

Sampling considerations – print

If your topic involves the analysis of newspapers or magazines there are certain features that you will need to be aware of in order to construct a good sample.

1. Editorial stance – Many publications will have a particular political or social stance that may affect the way that they portray certain issues.
2. Target audience – The intended readership will also affect this coverage, not just in terms of appealing to particular beliefs or attitudes, but also in the type of coverage that an issue may receive. For example, if you are studying the reputation of a particular multinational company, there will be publications that feature that company in terms of 'headline-grabbing' stories or events and there will be others that place more emphasis on financial performance.
3. Publication dates – The regularity with which the text is published will also affect content. You could reasonably expect a daily newspaper to be slightly different from one that is published at weekends only, perhaps in terms of the depth of coverage.

   Daily newspapers will have their own considerations. If you are looking at sporting coverage for example, you may need to consider the differences daily (given that a lot of sporting events take place on weekends). There may well be differences in the amount and type of coverage during the build-up to the event compared to the post-event reaction and analysis.
4. Circulation – The reach of the publication will also be important, and this will include the three factors above. You could reasonably expect a regional publication to vary in editorial stance, target audience, frequency of publication and depth of coverage of particular issues from those of a national or international publication.

Analysis considerations – print

As we've mentioned, deciding on your unit of analysis (the text that you will analyse) will depend very much on your hypotheses. If you are looking at newspapers, some of the things you may want to consider are whether you treat an entire article as a unit or whether you break this down. For example, you may consider only the headline and the first leader paragraph to be of interest, or you may break the article down into separate paragraphs.

You may also consider whether you are simply interested in articles that appear on the front page or whether the whole newspaper is of interest, bearing in mind that this will also contain in-depth articles, opinion pieces, editorials and letters.

You may also want to give some thought to the use of images that accompany a piece of text, particularly in a newspaper article.

If you are looking at the representation of a phenomenon in a fictional genre, will you need to consider all of the relevant texts or can you break this down to make a representative sample – for example, by only using the top ten best-sellers (although this may introduce some bias in itself)?

Sample considerations – television

Broadcasting also has a set of considerations when considering sampling issues, some of which are broadly analogous to those for print media.

1. Editorial stance – Some television networks have particular idiosyncrasies in their programming and editorial style. The nature and depth of news coverage may depend on the ethos of the editors (authoritative and austere, or more populist); but another consideration may be whether the station is publicly funded or commercial.
2. Target audience – Particular networks or particular programmes will appeal to a particular audience. News coverage in particular will vary according to time of day (see below) and length of programme (bulletin or in-depth analysis). Programming and content will also vary according to the nature of the network (some are subscription-only while others may be far more widely available).
3. Broadcast time – Time of day will clearly have implications for programming. Particular times may be assumed mainly to be aimed at a specific audience demographic – people who are working from home, children, insomniacs – and this will affect not only the types of programme broadcast (for instance, if you are looking at commercial channels and their advertising), but also the content of programmes that appear regularly throughout any given day, particularly news broadcasts. For example, in the UK

there is a regulation that deals with what is known as the *watershed*. This is a cut-off point (currently 9.00 p.m.) after which it is assumed that fewer children will be watching. This has implications for the types of programming acceptable by the regulators, as well as the types of adverts (and products/services) and, to some extent at least, the nature and imagery of news broadcasts.

4. Reach – Again, related to target audience and broadly analogous to circulation, some networks or specific channels are available regionally, while others are available nationally or internationally. This will also be influenced by whether they are transmitted terrestrially or via satellite or cable.

Analysis considerations – broadcast

Analysing broadcast material can be very complex given the interplay of script and visual material. If you are looking at a news broadcast for example, you will need to think about how to break this into units of analysis. Where does one segment end and another begin? In a recent project looking at the coverage of the 2003 war in Iraq, the coders spent many merry hours agonising over the differences between a one-minute piece to camera by a journalist and a ten-second introduction by the studio anchor.

The imagery in a piece of television obviously provides a great deal of the context and careful thought is needed to take this into account.

Yeah Ok, but how do I DO it?

The process of conducting a content analysis essentially involves designing a questionnaire, except that, instead of people answering the questions (about how old they are, for example), you will get the answers from the text that you are analysing (for example, which newspaper the article comes from). This is known as a *coding sheet* and the answers can be very simple or very complicated, depending on your research questions or hypotheses.

Each unit of analysis (news story, television broadcast, etc.) will need a separate coding sheet. You can either spend time in a darkened room surrounded by piles of paper ticking off each attribute of the text, or you can construct an electronic version of your coding sheet and enter data straight to the computer for subsequent analysis.

Constructing a coding sheet

As in a questionnaire, you can divide a coding sheet into discrete sections.

The first is analogous to the *demographics* section. This will analyse elements of the medium itself that you feel will make a difference to the ways in which the issue is covered. Some things you might want to look at are:

1. When and where – Year; date or day of the week; time of broadcast. Does coverage change over time? What publication or television outlet the piece appeared in.
2. Prominence – Word length or timing. Position in the publication (lead story, editorial, letter) or in the broadcast (lead story or further down the running order).
3. Context – What other material surrounds the piece you are interested in? For example, what are the themes in the other stories on a front page, or what are the preceding and following items in a news broadcast?

The second major section will directly concern your research questions/hypotheses. This will need extremely careful planning (and good justification in your methodology section).

Again, some things will be simple counts, but others may involve the identification of themes and language that will need to be operationally defined to avoid straying into the realms of more qualitative analysis.

1. Simple counts:

   Speakers – who gets to speak directly?
   Sources – who is quoted (and how are they identified)?
   Themes – what are the key themes or messages running through the text?

2. Linguistic modifiers

   Labels – are there recurring labels used for a particular group or issue?

Language of the headline – are there any recurring words (for example, those that are particularly emotive)?

3. Imagery

What are the most common images that accompany the issue?

Piloting

Content analysis can be very time-consuming so it is important that you get it right. It's worth taking a small sample of texts and testing your coding sheet before you begin the entire analysis.

Check that your coding sheet works and that you haven't missed anything important. As a tip, it can be useful to have an 'other' section so that you can fill in details of occurrences that were unexpected and then add this to the final version of the coding sheet.

Remember that all categories must be mutually exclusive, i.e. something that is coded can only be coded in one way. Often there will be a blurring of the categories so you should take the time to decide which category an example might fit into now.

It is worth experimenting at this stage *to some extent*.

The final version of the coding sheet is one that you must stick to. You must follow the rules of quantitative methods – this is not an exploratory method, and you cannot change the coding sheet as you go through the final analysis.

Inter-coder reliability

A final, and essential, check on your coding sheet is that another person would code a text in the same way that you have. This will avoid accusations of subjectivity, but will also help you construct the final version so that categories are clear and mutually exclusive.

Many pieces of published content analysis work will include a mathematical check on inter-coder reliability that quantifies the amount of agreement between different coders (see, for example, Wimmer and Dominick, 2006). As part of an introduction to this technique it's not strictly necessary, but it really is worth taking a selection of examples of your text and get at least one other person to code them.

Get together with your other coders and compare notes.

Analysis

Since this is a purely descriptive method, the good news is that the analysis you will use will be descriptive statistics.

Frequencies and cross-tabulation will be sufficient to describe your findings and can prove very powerful.

Chapter 10 shows you how to run these simple tests and interpret the results.

CHAPTER 8

Piloting

Now that you have a research question and have the most cunning, comprehensive, cute questionnaire ever created, you may feel that you're ready to get out there and begin collecting vast amounts of data.

Don't.

Not yet.

A *vital* stage to go through now is the process of piloting – testing the questionnaire. This chapter aims to explain why this process is important, what you might look out for and how you might go about it.

There are several reasons for going through this testing process, but the most crucial is that you do not waste all your time and effort distributing this first version, collecting the data, entering the results and completing the analyses, only to find out that the questionnaire doesn't measure what you intended it to, or that respondents have misunderstood the questions, or that you wish you had asked different questions altogether.

Although this process may seem laborious it is designed to save you time and effort in the long run. Often you will only get one shot at collecting your data so it's important to get it right.

Piloting the pilot questionnaire

There are several parts of the questionnaire that you can check as a group even before the piloting process begins.

Question wording

- Is the wording of each question clear and unambiguous?
- Is each question asking exactly what you want it to?
- Can each question be answered simply and easily by the respondent?
- Do all closed-ended questions have the complete range of possible answers? (Remember *Other*.)

Instructions

- Is it clear to the respondent how they should answer questions (circling the answer, ticking a box, etc.)?
- Is there any ambiguity about how the respondent can answer the question? (Should they give only one answer or can they make multiple responses? Do they have to rank responses in order of preference or frequency?)
- If the questionnaire is to be printed double-sided, are there clear instructions to turn over? (Trust us – it can be disastrous if they only complete one side of the page.)
- If the questionnaire is designed to be split into relevant sections, is this clear? (For example: *If Yes, go to Question 7. If No, go to Question 10.*)

Presentation

- Does the questionnaire look professional?
- Is it clear which answers relate to which questions?
- Are there typographical errors?
- Does it look scary/baffling/time-consuming?

Always check for typographical errors/spelling mistakes/poor grammar. If the questionnaire is in English but this is not your first language, make sure you get a classmate to check it over.

If the questionnaire is in your first language, get someone else who speaks the same language to check it (and perhaps even translate it).

Courtesy

- Have you explained who you are and the purpose of the questionnaire (without giving too much away, of course)?
- Have you guaranteed anonymity?
- Have you made it clear that respondents should not feel obliged to answer anything they do not wish to?
- Have you thanked your respondents for taking part?
- How long does it take to complete?

Piloting the questionnaire for real

Checking the instrument

If you are working in groups within a class, hand out copies of your questionnaire to the other groups and offer to complete their questionnaire in return. If you are working individually or in a group outside the class situation, use friends or flatmates.

It's worth giving out at least twenty questionnaires; this will give you a wider range of respondents and will also provide you with some data to test. If you're in a class, get everyone to do it (and return the favour). This is a useful exercise for all concerned, not just to check the questionnaires themselves, but also to look at how other groups may have designed their layout and phrased their questions.

Ask them to make notes on your draft version about anything they were unclear about or any other comments they might have. Explain that their comments are welcome. Take them seriously, but you don't have to adhere to all of them.

Go through the checklists above and see if the pilot sample has raised any issues that you might not have thought of as a group.

You may well be surprised at people's responses. Often a question that seems the epitome of simplicity to you and your team can be completely unintelligible to others. Often people will respond in an unexpected (or bizarre) fashion. One of the most common problems we have found is that people will give more than one answer unless explicitly told not to. This can cause all sorts of complications at the coding and data entry stage and so it's best avoided or anticipated now.

Checking the coding

Now that you have some pilot data you can begin to create the SPSS coding frame. This is where the fun begins. Work as a group to do this so that everyone knows how the data are entered (and therefore how to interpret the results).

- Does everyone agree on how to code each question? This is known as 'intercoder reliability' and is a good check on the validity of your questionnaire. Remember that the best research aims to be easily replicated – that is, someone else, in another classroom, country or continent, would come up with the same way of processing the data from your questionnaire as you have (or at least see how and why you did what you did).

- Are there any problematic questions? For example, has any respondent given more than one answer to a particular question? If so, think about how you might deal with this. Have any respondents given unusual or unanticipated answers? If so, you may want to include these answers in your list for closed-ended questions.
- Does a particular question remain unanswered more than once? This may be a result of poor or ambiguous wording, or it could reflect the fact that your pilot sample lacked the knowledge or experience to provide an answer. Decide if this will be a problem for your full sample. Remember that this may in fact be a finding in itself (see below).
- Can any open-ended questions be quantified? If you have used open-ended questions or those that allow the respondent to give fuller answers (e.g. *If Yes, please briefly explain why*), you can look for frequently occurring responses or patterns of responses that you may be able to put into SPSS. It may be better to wait until you have the full data set before doing this, but it's something that is worth thinking about at this stage.

Checking the findings
Another useful outcome of this process is that it will give you pilot data to play with. This may give you a hint of what to expect from the full sample and will also help you refine your questionnaire to get the most out of it. Although these results are clearly from a very limited sample, they may provide some food for thought about other questions that you may include in the final version. (See Chapter 10 to learn how to run the simple tests below.)

1. Run frequencies on everything. This will help you identify any redundant questions or those that may need to be re-phrased to give a wider range of responses (for example, if respondents from your pilot sample all answered *Strongly Agree* to a particular question).
2. Go back to your original hypotheses. Test these using simple crosstabs or correlations where appropriate.

Again, despite the limited sample, you may find things that don't work out as expected. This is not necessarily a problem; negative

findings (i.e. ones that do not support your hypotheses) are still important (see Chapters 10 and 11) and may even turn out to be one of the
most interesting things about your project. This may also prompt the
'But what if . . .' question. This is one of the key elements of research –
trying to explain or account for findings, both 'positive' (i.e. in the direction you predicted) and 'negative' (i.e. completely baffling).

It turns out that X appears to have absolutely no effect on Y. This
may be due to limited numbers of responses or it may be the beginnings of a more robust result.

But what if it's not X that has the effect, but Z. Why not include a
question about Z in the final version? Just to check. For example, a
student project on alcohol consumption and expenditure found that,
while males and females claimed to drink roughly equal amounts, the
women appeared to spend considerably less on a night out. Including
a question on whom they bought drinks FOR shed some light on this
(and possibly suggested that chivalry is not dead).

Making use of the pilot

Make a note of these discoveries and discussions as you go along.
They can be useful in the final project report when discussing the
rationale behind what you decided to do in the full version. They will
also help clarify things to yourself and the group members when you
come to describe the process weeks or months later. ('Why on earth
did we do that?')

Think about ways in which you might use the (limited) results of
your pilot questionnaire, perhaps even including these data in your
report of the final project.

Piloting the process

Think about the practicalities of administering the pilot questionnaire as well. All of these lessons will prove useful when conducting
the final project.

- Did the questionnaire take too long to complete?
- Did I run out of pencils?
- What problems did I have in recruiting respondents?

CHAPTER 9

Special Audiences – Work with Children

Both of us have experience of doing research with children and with families. Empirical research with children can be very rewarding and is popular with some students, so we have included this separate chapter on it. However, we should say at the outset: don't do research with children unless you feel confident about dealing with them and their caretakers directly. Children are a special group, requiring special techniques, and they are also potentially vulnerable to being upset emotionally or to being adversely affected educationally. Parents and teachers too can be inconvenienced and annoyed by researchers who haven't designed their project with children carefully, and who haven't consulted the relevant adults in advance about practicalities or explained their research goals.

Safeguards and consent

You will need a whole variety of safeguards in setting up a project with children, and unless you already have some inside experience of doing this – e.g. experience of working in a playgroup, or as a volunteer with a Cub or Brownie group, or in a former professional career (as some students do have) – don't attempt such research in a short-term project. Sometimes it's possible to do a project with children because you have a parent, or partner, who is a teacher, who can help you. A dissertation project, especially a three-year PhD, makes such a project more feasible because working with children, even more than with other human subjects, requires a great deal of prior planning and organisation before you carry it out. Before you embark on such a project make sure you do the following:

- Check with your tutor or supervisor about university regulations with regard to work with human subjects generally and children in particular.
- Check your proposed project with the university, faculty or department ethics committee.

- Make sure you have followed the advice given below about parental permission, school permission and children's own consent before you start.
- If there are likely to be problems with any of this, think about revising your project. For instance, if you can't gain access to children easily, think about asking *adult* subjects about their experiences and memories of childhood, or look at the ways in which children are represented in the media.[1]

Approaching children and families

The first step is to find some children – obviously! Standard approaches for student projects are via personal contacts. If you already know some teachers, or families, try them first. They may enable you to contact other teachers and parents. If you don't have personal contacts with access to children, it will be a lot harder to set up a study for a short-term student project. It is different with more formal, professional research.

Always contact children via their caretakers, never directly.

That said, make sure that the children themselves want to help you. If they don't, it's their right to withdraw and their parents shouldn't override them. Don't use children if they are unwilling, even if their elders are willing. The discrepancy between children's willingness to take part in TV programmes and their parents' willingness to let them do so was one of the strongest findings of our *Consenting Children?* study. On the whole, parents thought it was OK; children didn't. Children have the right to opt out. This should be made clear to teachers and parents, and to the children, when you introduce your research to them.

If you approach children via their schools (the easiest way of accessing a number of children), this must be done through the head

---

[1] See for instance M. M. Davies (2004) 'Innocent victims/active citizens: children and media war coverage' in A. Biressi and H. Nunn (eds), *Mediactive: Media War* (London: Lawrence and Wishart), pp. 55–66, and C. Carter and M. M. Davies (2005) ' "A fresh peach is easier to bruise": Children and traumatic news', in S. Allan (ed.), *Journalism: Critical Issues*, Maidenhead and New York: Open University Press, pp. 224–35.

teacher. If he/she is willing, be guided by their advice as to how best to proceed in setting up the study. The first stage is to write a letter to the parents, to be sent via the school, asking their permission. An example is given below. The simplest way to make sure that you don't involve the school in a lot of time-consuming chasing up of these letters is to say at the end:

> 'If we don't hear from you by the end of next week (*or whatever date the school suggests*), we will assume that you have granted your permission for your child to take part.'

The letter needs to come via the school, on their headed notepaper, so that parents are reassured that this is a proper educational activity. When you write to schools or parents yourselves, write on university headed notepaper and make sure with your head of school that this is OK. An example (of a parental letter) from a recent project carried out by Máire Messenger Davies is given on pp. 116–17.

Common issues of concern

Below is a checklist of issues that arise when working with children. Again, if these look too daunting, think about revising your project as suggested above.

> **Ethics**: Check that you've explored the ethical procedures for setting up your project with your university or department's ethics committee.
>
> **Police vetting**: With schools, you may find that you have to be checked by the police before you are allowed in to work with children. Don't be offended by this. It is a standard safeguard. An alternative is to ask your contact teachers to administer your questionnaire for you, but this is less satisfactory than doing it yourself. It is always good to have a discussion with children afterwards, to find out what they thought about the exercise.
>
> **Consent**: Make sure you have parental consent by the use of a standard letter such as the example given above.
>
> **Will it work?** Other issues are:
>
> - Issues of comprehension – can they understand?
> - Issues of 'affect' – will they be nervous, upset, irritated?

Format of permission letter to parents, sent via children's school

CHILDREN AND HUMOUR STUDY

Centre for Media Research, University of Ulster

Dear Parents/Guardians

We are a team of university researchers from the Centre for Media Research in the University of Ulster, who are taking part in an international study on children's humour organised by the International Institute for the Study of Young People and Media (IZI) in Munich. On 27 and 28 June we are visiting your school as part of this study. During our visit we want to show children aged between 8 and 11 (years 4 to 7) some children's television from different countries and to assess how the children respond to this. For this we need your permission for your child to take part. We hope you will agree as we think it will be an enjoyable experience.

The study will involve showing five clips of humorous TV material, all taken from children's programmes, and containing nothing unsuitable, to small groups of between 8 and 10 children and assessing their reactions. Children will be asked to operate a 'fun-o-meter' (like a computer game joystick) while they are watching (and laughing, we hope) and we will be talking to them about the programmes after they have seen them. We also want to film the children's reactions. The selected programme clips are: Pink Panther (USA); Angela Anaconda ('global'); Tabaluga TV (Germany); Open a Door (South Africa); Hidden Camera (Israel); Wallace and Gromit (UK/Ireland). We will also be talking about other humorous programmes the children might want to refer to in the post-viewing discussions.

Accordingly, we are writing to request your permission to involve your child in this study, which will take place in the school on 27 and 28 June 2005. Although we will require information about the children's names, all responses will be reported anonymously, and will be seen only by the school and the research team.

Please could you indicate your willingness, or otherwise, for your child to participate by filling in and returning the tear-off slip below to your child's teacher. If the school does not receive this slip back from you by 20 May, they will assume that you have granted your permission.

If you have any questions with regard to this study, please contact the school office directly.

Thank you very much in anticipation.

Yours sincerely,
Máire Messenger Davies (Professor),
Director, Centre for Media Research, University of Ulster at Coleraine.

Child's name: _____   Parent/
                                   Guardian Name: _____

I DO/DO NOT WISH MY CHILD TO TAKE PART IN THE CHILDREN
AND HUMOUR STUDY
(Please delete as appropriate)

- Issues of behaviour – what do you do if they misbehave? This is where the double safeguards of piloting first (even if only with some children you know from next door) and having a teacher or authority figure in the room with you when you carry out your survey or task are absolutely vital.
- Issues in qualitative research tasks: What kinds of materials do you use? Playful tasks such as the role-playing exercise used in the *Dear BBC* study, where several groups of five or six children had to be 'TV schedulers' and choose six out of thirty-two programme titles for a special children's schedule, are both educationally interesting (involving tasks such as negotiation, discussion, consensus-building, decision-making and critical judgements) and enjoyable. The children were given colour-coded badges and coloured cards with programme titles to organise, which made the task more playful.
- Issues of interpretation: what on earth are they talking about? This can be a problem in qualitative data – although it is still good to get some qualitative data (talk or written comments) if you can. Questionnaire formats, where children

simply have to choose an option (tick or circle a box), make subsequent interpretation a lot easier – another reason for using this valuable research tool.

- Issues of personal involvement: everybody has been a child – what's your own agenda here? Don't assume that your child-hood experiences will be matched by other children's, and don't assume – if you have children – that this makes you an expert on other people's children. It doesn't! However, it is a very useful experience to have in terms of feeling more con-fident and comfortable around children.

Designing research with children

Some research questions are answerable with children, some are not. This may be to do with issues of 'suitability' (what you will be allowed to ask children); it is also to do with what children are capable of understanding and doing, which varies markedly, particularly with age, but also for other reasons. It's also important to find tasks that will be enjoyable and meaningful for them to do, otherwise they will be bored, unhappy and uncooperative; unlike adults (who tend to want to please researchers) children will *show* their dissatisfaction –this is another threat to **validity**. Even more than with adult subjects, the methodologies you choose for research with children need to be closely linked to your research question. And this question must be a feasible one.

Feasible media research questions for student projects with children

- Questions about taste: what children like.
- Questions about specific media products aimed at children, e.g. *Harry Potter*, Playstations (but beware being exclusionary – what about the kids in the class whose families can't afford these?)
- Questions aimed at children over the age of seven, who can (usually) read and write at least a little; who can understand instructions; and who will be accustomed to relating to adults other than their parents and relatives.

- Questions about differences between boys and girls.
- Questions about differences between younger (7–9) and older (10–12) children.
- Questions about media habits.
- Questions about advertising and products.
- Questions about children's opinions – including politics and cultural attitudes.
- Questions about their knowledge of the world and the media's contribution to this.
- Questions which enable them to demonstrate skills and knowledge that they are confident about and/or proud of. Research into popular culture often falls into this category, as even the most non-academic children can have specialised knowledge about TV or about video games. Popular culture also often transcends ethnic, religious and other cultural differences – hence it is easier to design questionnaires, or other research tasks, which you know will be broadly familiar to most children.

Non-feasible research questions with children: What not to ask

- Questions about sex and violence (parents and teachers are likely to object).
- Questions which require them to reveal socio-economic status (parental income) or other personal information about their families.
- Questions which require them to challenge their parents' value systems (e.g. about religion or ethnicity).
- Questions about pre-school, pre-literate or infant children. Research with this group is fascinating but requires highly specialised research techniques: possible if you are a psychology student in a good developmental psychology programme, less so if you are not. However it might be possible to address the questions you are interested in by surveying their parents.
- Questions which require children's extended effort and concentration over long periods of time.
- Questions which are disruptive of their routines and lives, whether in school or home.

- Questions which require them to behave badly. (Some classic experiments with children which attempted to measure the effects of media violence by requiring young children to show aggression towards other children, or toys, are highly suspect ethically – and less valid for this reason.)

Feasible research methods with children

- Short questionnaires (not more than 20–30 simple questions).
- Visual questionnaires (especially for under eight-year-olds) such as the 'smiley face' technique (see Figure 9.2).
- Three-point scales rather than five-point Likert scales (e.g. 'agree; disagree; not sure').
- Free expression sections: 'What do you think?'
- Drawings – but you need to be clear about what you want the drawings to express.
- Structured tasks – e.g. the scheduling task from *Dear BBC*.
- Group work which can be done in a classroom.
- Using simple technology with which children are familiar. Some computer programs can be used if both you and the children are familiar with them, and if they answer specific research questions. It is unwise to ask children to use technology that either they, or you, or both of you, haven't used before. However, useful work with children and technology has been done with more ethnographic approaches where the researcher has time to get to know children in their family setting, and where there is time to sort out technological difficulties if necessary (see e.g. S. Livingstone, *Young People and New Media*, 2002).

Questionnaires for children

Despite what you might think, questionnaires are a good tool for doing research with children, as long as they are appropriately designed. They have a number of advantages:

- They are anonymous.
- They include every child.
- They are carried out by each child individually and hence are less subject to peer pressure in answering.

- They are orderly: working with children in sociable and interactive groups is very enjoyable, but risky if you don't know the children and don't feel confident about keeping order. If every child is working busily on a questionnaire, it is easier for a young, unfamiliar inexperienced researcher to manage the situation (but always with a teacher or caretaker in the room with you, of course).
- Questionnaires are 'grown up'. Children are likely to be aware that adults are sometimes consulted in this way in public opinion polls and market research. The questionnaire is an adult research instrument, and children do like to be treated and consulted in an adult manner. This, too, is conducive to good order.
- They permit private responses – unlike group discussions, where again peer pressure may mean that some children say nothing, and others go along with the more dominant members of the group. In a questionnaire, answers are more likely to be the child's own views, not somebody else's. We found very strong evidence of the value of questionnaire privacy in some research we did for the Broadcasting Standards Commission (*Consenting Children?*, 2001). Parents and children were given the same questionnaire about children appearing in adult TV programmes. For every question, the responses of adults and children were different, with adults being more likely to approve of children appearing on TV than children were. This was a clear validation of the research hypothesis that parents can't necessarily speak for their children when it comes to 'consent' – at least to appearing on television. Of course, parents must be consulted when you are working with children, but it should not be assumed that parents and children are always going to agree (see Figure 9.1).

Designing a questionnaire for children

A questionnaire for children should not be long and it should be very simple. We give an example from Máire Messenger Davies' *Fake, Fact and Fantasy* in Figure 9.2. This was given to seventy-eight children between the ages of eight and fourteen years and none of them had problems reading or answering it. However, children younger than this might have had difficulty, and if we had included younger

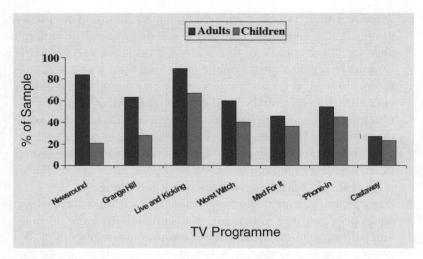

Figure 9.1. From Davies and Mosdell 2001: *Consenting Children?* Differences between parents' and children's responses to questions about children appearing on television. Respondents were asked 'I would like [child's version]/I would like my children [adults' version] to appear on (name of programme)': 'Agree; disagree; not sure'. The graph shows the 'agree' responses. (Base: 53 adults, 78 children.)

children in our sample, we would have made the questionnaire shorter and had a visual version. Some children in a whole-class group of older children may also have literacy problems. These should be identified in advance, and then a classroom assistant or extra researcher can be laid on to help them.

Visual techniques

With a group of younger children who can't read or write very easily, a usual technique is to read out the questionnaire to them, page by page, with each question on a different page and they all turn over the page together. Visual symbols for 'agree'; 'disagree' and 'not sure' (such as the 'smiley face') are a standard technique and can work very well. All the children have to do is to tick the relevant 'face'. Other visual techniques such as choosing between two or more pictures, or recognition of pictures of characters from programmes or films, can also be used. Work with children can produce some very enjoyable and imaginative solutions to research method problems, so don't be

If you wish hard when you blow out you birthday candles, your wish will come true.

True   Not true   Not sure

If people on TV adventure shows have a fight, they don't really hurt each other.

True   Not true   Not sure

There needs to be violence on TV to make the programmes exciting.

True   Not true   Not sure

Figure 9.2 Questionnaires for young children: the smiley face technique. 'Questions about "real and not real" ' from Máire Messenger Davies (1997), *Fake, Fact and Fantasy: Children's Understanding of Television Reality*, Mahwah, NJ: Lawrence Erlbaum, pp. 168–73.

Programs like 'Full House' and 'The Cosby Show' happen in somebody's real house.

True   Not true   Not sure

TV ads make toys and candy look much nicer than they really are.

True   Not true   Not sure

Superman and Batman aren't really flying in the movies; it's a trick.

True   Not true   Not sure

Figure 9.2 (continued)

put off by all the needs for safeguards. You can have a lot of creative enjoyment with this kind of work.

Questions can also be administered via computer programs, but as we've said already, don't do anything with technology unless you are *super-confident* that it will work for both you and the children and their teachers/parents.

An alternative with non-literate children is to interview them individually and fill in their spoken answers, but this is very time-consuming and again, you may run into ethical difficulties if you are with a child unsupervised.

BSC STUDY: CHILDREN'S AND TEENAGERS' QUESTIONNAIRE

(*Information about the project had already been given in a separate letter to the families, so there was no need to put an introductory paragraph at the top of this questionnaire. We also did not use the leading word 'Consenting', so did not put the title of our research on this questionnaire.*)

My name is:

(*this was a family project where names had to be identified, but the children and families were still kept anonymous in our report to the BSC*)

I am _____ years old

Please look at the statements below and then circle one of the answers opposite;

1. I watch TV
a) less than one hour a day
b) 2–3 hours per day
c) more than 3 hours a day
d) never

2. I read books or magazines
a) less than one hour a day
b) 2–3 hours a day
c) more than 3 hours a day
d) never

3. I listen to the radio

a) less than one hour a day
b) 2–3 hours a day
c) more than 3 hours a day
d) never

4. I go to the theatre

a) at least once a month
b) six or more times a year
c) two or three times a year
d) once a year
e) less than once a year
f) never

5. I go to the cinema

a) at least once a month
b) six or more times a year
c) two or three times a year
d) once a year
e) less than once a year
f) never

6. I go to the library

a) at least once a month
b) six or more times a year
c) two or three times a year
d) once a year
e) less than once a year
f) never

My favourite TV programme is (name one):

_____

My favourite children's TV programme is (name one):

_____

My favourite TV personality is (name one):

_____

Now look at the statements below and then circle one of the answers opposite;

| **I watch TV with my parents** | Regularly | Sometimes | Never |

I watch TV with my parents   Regularly   Sometimes   Never

I watch TV with my brothers and sisters   Regularly   Sometimes   Never

I watch TV with my friends   Regularly   Sometimes   Never

I watch daytime TV   Regularly   Sometimes   Never

I am allowed to watch TV until   8 o'clock   9 o'clock
10 o'clock   Later

I talk about TV programmes with (circle more than one if you want)   My parents
My brothers and sisters
My friends
No one
Don't know

What TV programmes do you watch with your parents? (list up to three, or leave blank if you don't watch any with them)

_____

What TV programmes do you watch with your brothers and sisters? (list up to three, or leave blank if you don't watch any with them)

_____

What TV programmes do you watch with your friends? (list up to three, or leave blank if you don't watch any with them)

_____

Name a TV programme that you are NOT allowed to watch:

_____

Look at the statements below and then circle one of the answers opposite

1. I would like to act in a realistic drama programme like _Grange Hill_	Agree	Not Sure	Disagree
2. I would like to be a contestant in a game show like _Mad for It_	Agree	Not Sure	Disagree
3. I would like to act in a fantasy story like _The Worst Witch_	Agree	Not Sure	Disagree
4. I would like to be in the audience on a magazine show like _Live and Kicking_	Agree	Not Sure	Disagree
5. I would like to be in a real life documentary like _Castaway_	Agree	Not Sure	Disagree
6. I would like to be on a phone-in on Radio One	Agree	Not Sure	Disagree
7. I would like to be a reporter on a news programme like _Newsround_	Agree	Not Sure	Disagree

Given only one choice, what kind of TV programme would you most like to be in? (Say why if you can)

What sort of TV programmes should young children NOT be allowed to watch? (List up to three if you can)

Is there anything else that you would like to say?

As you can see, we used the three-point scale rather than the five-point scale for our 'opinion questions' (and did the same with the parents' questionnaire, for ease of comparison). However, there are a number of other places in the questionnaire where there are up to six options (e.g. TV viewing). The questionnaire includes both closed (multiple-choice) and open-ended questions. The children who answered this took about half an hour to do it. Perhaps you can think of ways in which it could be adapted for other uses, or improved. Also, how you would code it.

Research with children: points to remember

1. Making contact and setting up the study: as we've said, use local schools, parents, teachers, etc. whom you already know. Convenience samples are the only ones that will work for a student project with children because of the trust issue, as well as the limits on time and resources which are inevitable with student work. However, you can still use your 'convenient' schools as a valid 'population' if your research question is sufficiently specific (see Chapter 4).
2. Parental permission.
3. School may require police vetting.
4. If you are showing film, television or online material, offer parents and teachers the chance to view it first. They may not want to do so and may trust you to choose suitable material for their children, especially if the material is uncontentious. However, if some of the material *is* contentious (because it has led to adult complaints,

as in the case of our 2001 BSC study *Consenting Children?*) it is wise to cover yourself by asking adults to sign a permission form that it's OK for their children to see it, if they don't want to preview it themselves.[2]

5. If you are working in schools, visit the school and check out the rooms and resources you will be using first. Make sure all equipment works; make sure all teachers involved know when it is you want their children to take part. Make sure all teachers involved have seen your research instruments, including questionnaires, interview schedules, etc. Give them the opportunity to revise wording, etc., e.g. if language needs to be simplified.

6. When conducting the research, whether with a class of children or with children in their homes, have the relevant authority figure (teacher or parent) with you in the room; this is a legalistic requirement, as well as a sensible practical one. In a classroom, it's better for there to be at least two researchers too.

That said, do not let teachers or parents help or interfere with the administration of the research procedures once you've started. It is the children's views you want, not the adults'. It is always necessary to impress on both the children and their caretakers/teachers that research is *not a test*. There are no right or wrong answers to a research questionnaire or a research task. Researchers are just as interested in non-answers, or strange answers, as in what people might see as more conventional, 'correct' answers. If adults interfere with children's performance (it's OK if all they want to do is help with spelling, or get another piece of paper), this destroys the **internal validity** of the research procedures and all your careful preparation will have gone for nothing. Teachers and parents naturally can be very keen for the children in their care to make a good impression; researchers don't

---

[2] In the case of *Consenting Children?* we used the requirement for parental vetting as a positive element in the research design: we showed all the material to parents before showing it to the whole family, including the children, and we were interested to see whether the parental comments, approval or disapproval, were borne out by the children's reactions when they saw what their parents had already seen. In many cases, there were very revealing differences between the two viewing sessions, and the parents were surprised by their children's responses.

care about this. Indeed, we learn more from the mistakes and difficulties people have than we do from perfect responses. If all the answers to a questionnaire or research task are 'right', we run into the danger of producing a '**ceiling effect**'. Everybody gives the same answers, so there is no **variance** and nothing to measure, and no variety of scores to help evaluate differences between different people and different responses.

In summary

It may seem, after reading all this, that doing research with children is not worth the trouble because of all the safeguards and provisos you have to remember. However, as we've said, if you already have good contacts (with schools, or groups such as Cubs, Brownies or other youth groups) and with professional adults who will 'stand surety' for you, and help you with all the practicalities, doing work with children is one of the most enjoyable forms of research there can be. Be very clear about your research question and hypothesis, and, as we've said, steer clear of controversial or potentially upsetting topics: focus on what they *like* (or dislike), what they *think* and what they *do*, and you cannot go far wrong. Always pilot your research instrument, whether a questionnaire or a task such as the scheduling task, and consult your contact teacher or parent about its wording, length, practicality and so on. With children the practicalities ('The Six Ps' – see Chapter 5) are even more important than they are with other groups. Permission is a crucial one. Make sure you are safeguarded by following all the proper consent and ethical procedures; this is a factor in a very important seventh 'P' – Professionalism.

PART THREE

ANALYSIS: 'UNDERSTANDING IT'

CHAPTER 10

Data Analysis

Now that you have designed a questionnaire, selected a sample and collected some data, it's time to have a look at what you have found. Time for some excitement. But first, you have to enter the data into the computer so that you can perform all sorts of complicated counts and comparisons at the click of a button.

There are various software packages that will allow you to analyse your questionnaire data, but a user-friendly and very powerful option is SPSS. This chapter aims to introduce the SPSS environment. It assumes no previous knowledge of this software, and is by no means intended as a comprehensive guide.[1] This chapter is based on Version 12.0 of this software. If you are running a different version, then some of the windows may appear slightly different but the principles are basically the same.

It deals with entering data and running simple statistical tests, as well as covering some basic concepts of statistical probability.

Entering data

The first thing to notice when you have started SPSS is that there are two tabs at the bottom of the screen: *data view* and *variable view*.

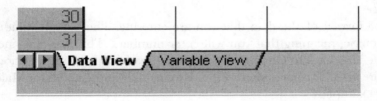

Variable view
This is the first step when entering your questionnaire data and basically allows you to set up the spreadsheet so that it reflects your questionnaire.

---

[1] A useful reference for statistics using SPSS is A. Field (2005) *Discovering Statistics Using SPSS*, London: Sage.

In *variable view*, each of the rows is a **variable** (something that varies) – usually a question – and the columns are attributes of that variable – what the variable is called, what the possible answers are, etc.

For example, your first question might be *'What is your gender?'* Hopefully, respondents will only have given one of two possible answers for this question – male or female. So, *Gender* is the variable, and *Male* and *Female* are *levels* of that variable.

You will notice that there are headings in the columns. Some of these columns require you to specify particular attributes, others are default values.

Name

Simply enough, what you decide to call the variable. There are certain limits to this – you can use alphanumeric characters (numbers and letters), but some symbols will not be accepted and there must be no spaces. Earlier versions of the software also had a character limit. As a rule of thumb, if you get an error message when you have entered a variable name, make sure there are no spaces or symbols and abbreviate the name if necessary.

To enter the name, click once inside the box under the *Name* column and type your choice of name (e.g. Gender).

When you click anywhere outside the box, a number of default values will be placed in the columns. Most of these will remain as they are.

Type

The format of the data that you are entering. The default value is numeric, meaning that you will enter numbers. This is useful since (referring back to Chapter 3) you have already coded your questionnaire in this format – where 1 stands for Female and 2 stands for Male, for example.

Width

A cosmetic point. The default is 8 – best leave it as it is.

Decimals

The number of decimal places that analyses will be calculated to. The default is 2. So, for example, if a calculation returns a result of 8.61235, SPSS will display 8.61.

Label

If you leave this box blank, any tables or graphs will display the variable name. This can be a useful place to extend the name so that it makes more sense or looks more aesthetically pleasing. You can use spaces and symbols for the variable label and the number of allowed characters is much higher.

Values

You must enter all of the values for each variable, i.e. all of the possible answers for each question, so that they are all available to you when you come to actually enter the data.

Click on the row of the variable you want to change under the column heading *Values*. Click the grey area with . . . in and a box will appear with *Value Labels*. Enter the *Value* (e.g. 1) in the first box and the *Label* (e.g. Female) in the second box. Click on *Add*. Click *OK* to finish once all values and labels are entered. If you need to change any values or value labels, select the value label from the list and change the value or the label by clicking and editing the *Value* or *Value Label* box and click *Change*.

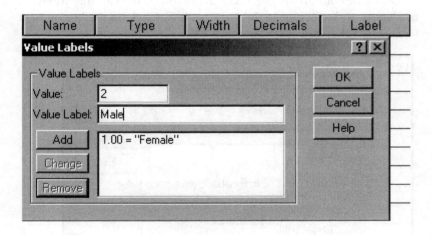

(This box appears when you click the grey . . . area of the first row under the column *Values*.)

A common mistake is to click *OK* before adding the final value. This will generate an error message and clicking on *OK* to that message will mean that the final value has not been added (you must click on *Add* before clicking *OK*).

Make sure that ALL possible answers appear in the box.

Missing

Another possible answer that people can give is not to answer at all. This is known as a *Missing Value* and can be very important. For example, if you find that a lot of people have not answered a particular question, it could indicate that the question was particularly sensitive (for example, many people are reluctant to give details of their income) or that the phrasing of the question meant that they felt unable or unqualified to answer it. This is another good reason for *piloting* the questionnaire (see Chapter 8) and testing the results of the pilot before collecting your 'real' data. Just as we have coded 1 for female and 2 for male, we need to assign a number for Missing. Usually we use a number that is unlikely to be reached in a list of possible answers. A common value for missing is 99. This is completely arbitrary, but you must make sure that the value will not be used as a code for any other answer.

Go to the column *Missing*. Click in the row of the variable you want to change and select using the grey . . . box. Click on the button next to *Discrete Values* and enter 99. Click *OK*.

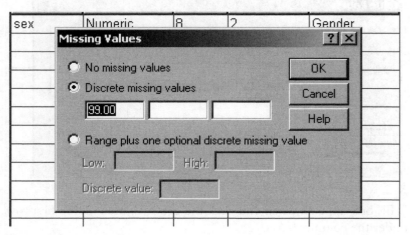

This box appears when you click the grey . . . area of the first row under the column *Missing*.

Columns

A cosmetic point. The default is 8 – best leave it as it is. This will change only if you stretch the column in *Data View*.

Align

A cosmetic point. The default is right – best leave it as it is.

Measure

The final thing to change. This refers to the type of data that the variable contains.

Remember that there are several levels of measurement (see Chapter 3). SPSS allows you to select *Nominal, Ordinal* and *Scale*. This may seem slightly confusing as much of your ordinal data will come from Likert scales.

As a tip, look at the icons next to each option.

- **Nominal** – not greater than, less than, higher in a list than, etc., just *different*.
- **Ordinal** – there is some order or progression in the way you have coded the data.
- **Scale** – refers to *Interval* or *Ratio* measurement, where the distance between points on the scale is always the same (as in distance, indicated by the ruler).

Click on the row of the variable you want to change under the column heading *Measure*. Click on the down arrow and a menu will appear containing three data types: *Scale; Ordinal; Nominal*. Select the one appropriate for your data.

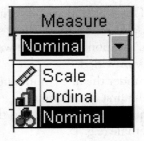

This box appears when you click the down arrow in the first row under the column *Measure*.

To recap, the headings you need to give some details for are:

1. name;
2. label (optional);
3. values;
4. missing;
5. measure.

The rest can safely be left as they are.

If you have made mistakes and want to remove variables, select the row by clicking inside the grey numbered area to the right of the screen and pressing delete.

You can also add new variables to the list by clicking in that area and going to the *Data* menu – select *Insert Variable*.

Once you have entered the specifications for every variable (basically, every question on your questionnaire), you are ready to begin entering data.

Put the kettle on and take a deep breath, this may take some time . . .

Data view

Click the tab at the bottom labelled *Data View*. This will bring you to a new blank screen, but you will notice that the columns now have variable names in them.

In *Data View*, each row is a person who filled out your questionnaire and each column is an attribute of that person – what their gender is, how old they are, etc.

Remember, it's a good idea to number each of your questionnaires before you input the data. This will stop you entering the same one twice and will also give a useful reference if there's something odd about a particular individual's responses or if you want to go back to any qualitative data that they provided.

Click in the top right box under the first column heading and enter the code for the answer on the first questionnaire.

For example, if the first question is Gender and the first person is female, enter the code for Female (e.g. 1).

If this is the first time that you have used SPSS, then you will see 1 on the screen. However, and this bit's magic, if you now click on the

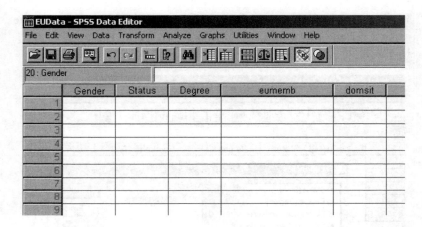

tiny button that looks like a luggage label (as in the above picture), that number will be transformed into the label that 1 stands for.

This also gives you the option of either entering the number directly or selecting from a drop-down menu for each variable.

Exploring the data

Once you have entered all your questionnaire data you can begin to look at what you have found.

The first step is always to run **frequencies** on every variable. This will give you some idea of what the data look like and will help you to spot any data entry mistakes (e.g. entering a 6 when you only have 5 values for that variable, or entering 55 instead of 5).

Frequencies

Frequencies are just simple counts of each level of a variable; for example, how many males and females you have in the sample.

1. From the *Analyse* menu –
    > *Descriptive Statistics* –
    >> *Frequencies* . . .
    This will bring up a box like the one shown on p. 142.
2. Select the variable you want to look at from the list on the left (click on it once so that it is highlighted).

3. Click on the right arrow. This will remove that variable from the first list and place it in the *Variable(s)*: list on the right.
4. Click *OK*.

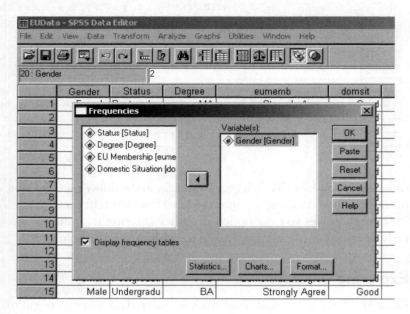

This will open up a new window in SPSS, titled *Output1 – SPSS Viewer*. Unless you close this window, each subsequent test will appear below the preceding one in this output window.

The frequency table from our EU example is shown below, for the variable 'gender'.

Statistics

Gender

N	Valid	20
	Missing	0

This first box simply shows what has gone into the test.

You can see that N = 20; that is, there are twenty cases in the table and that there are no missing values for this variable.

Gender

		Frequency	Per cent	Valid Per cent	Cumulative Per cent
Valid	Female	9	45.0	45.0	45.0
	Male	11	55.0	55.0	100.0
	Total	20	100.0	100.0	

This is the important part. You can see that there are five columns:

1. The values of the variable – *Female*, *Male* and the *Total*.
2. The *Frequency* (count) of these values – nine *Females* and eleven *Males* making a *Total* of twenty.
3. These counts expressed in *Per cent* – For example, nine *Females* out of a *Total* of twenty is 45.0 per cent.
4. These counts expressed as a *Valid Per cent* – this will differ from the *Per cent* only if you have any missing values. The *Per cent* expresses the numbers as a proportion of all of the people who returned your questionnaire. The *Valid Per cent* expresses these numbers as a proportion of all of the people who answered that particular question. The percentage that you choose to quote will depend on how many missing values you have. This is down to your judgement as a researcher.
5. A *Cumulative Per cent* – this adds up the valid percentages as you go down the columns. In this case, the first figure is 45.0. If you add the second figure (55.0) to this you get 100. This can be useful for combining levels of a particular variable – for example, if you want to know what proportion expressed some level of agreement to a particular statement you can combine the percentages for those who answered *Agree* with those who answered *Strongly Agree*.

Another useful tip is to click on the *Format . . .* button. The default is *Ascending values* that will display the frequencies in the order that the values were assigned. If you select *Descending counts*, this will display the values in descending order of frequency (i.e. the highest count first). This can save a great deal of time if you have a long list of values for a variable (for example, 'favourite TV programme').

Frequencies can be run on all variables, but there are other tests that depend on the data type that you have (nominal, ordinal, etc.). Two of the most useful are **Crosstabulation** and **Correlation**.

Crosstabulation

Crosstabulation (or Crosstabs) can be used with nominal data and any others. The table produced is basically the frequency of one variable within another variable – for example, how many female (Gender variable) undergraduates (Status variable) there were (as opposed to female postgraduates).

1. From the *Analyse* menu –
      Descriptive Statistics –
         Crosstabs . . .
   This will bring up a box like the one shown opposite.
2. Select one variable you want to look at from the list on the left (click on it once so that it is highlighted). Click on the upper right arrow. This will remove that variable from the first list and place it in the *Row(s)*: list on the right.
3. Select the second variable you want to look at and click on the second right arrow you see. This will remove that variable from the first list and place it in the *Column(s):* list on the right.
4. To change the display to percentages, click on the *Cells* . . . button at the bottom of the *Crosstabs* box. Click next to each of the *Row*, *Column* and *Total* boxes until there is a tick by each. Click *Continue*.

Click *OK*.

The way in which you assign variables to rows and columns does not affect the table's contents but it's good practice to assign the *Independent variable* (see Chapter 6) to the columns, just to make the table easier to read.

This will bring up a table like the one shown opposite.

The first thing to notice is that there are only nineteen cases included in this table. This is because Crosstabs do not include any Missing Values (for either variable).

In the table opposite we have females running across the first row – four undergraduate and five postgraduate making a total of nine. Males run across the second row – six undergraduates and four postgraduates, making a total of ten.

Because you are unlikely to have equal numbers for every variable, you should express the findings of the table using percentages. If, for example, you had 200 undergraduates and fifty postgraduates, simply

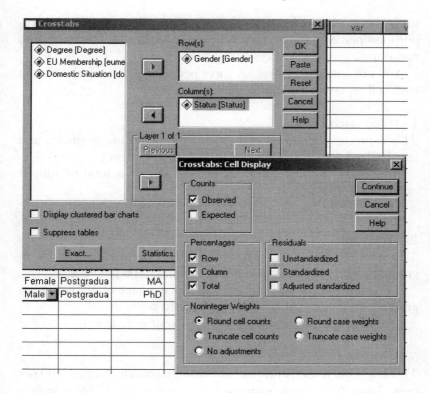

Gender * Status Cross-tabulation

			Status		
			Undergra-duate	Postgraduate	Total
Gender	Female	Count	4	5	9
		% within Gender	44.4%	55.6%	100.0%
		% within Status	40.0%	55.6%	47.4%
		% of Total	21.1%	26.3%	47.4%
	Male	Count	6	4	10
		% within Gender	60.0%	40.0%	100.0%
		% within Status	60.0%	44.4%	52.6%
		% of Total	31.6%	21.1%	52.6%
Total		Count	10	9	19
		% within Gender	52.6%	47.4%	100.0%
		% within Status	100.0%	100.0%	100.0%
		% of Total	52.6%	47.4%	100.0%

using the counts would obviously bias your results, but using the proportions (percentages) from each group will take the differences into account.

You will notice that there are three percentages below the count in each cell (square) of the table shown on p. 145.

1. Within gender
This expresses the count as a percentage of all of the males and females, and runs across the row to make 100 per cent.

If we take the first cell, four females out of a total of nine is expressed as 44.4 per cent.

Out of all the females, 44.4 per cent were undergraduates.

2. Within status
This expresses the count as a total of all the undergraduates and postgraduates and runs down the column to make 100 per cent.

The same four people expressed as a percentage of all the undergraduates – four out of ten – is shown as 40 per cent.

Out of all the undergraduates, 40 per cent were female.

3. Within total
This is less often used and basically runs diagonally to make 100 per cent. These four people expressed as a total of the whole sample – four out of nineteen – is shown as 21.1 per cent.

Out of all the people that we asked, 21.1 per cent were undergraduate and female.

To take the females and undergraduates example, think of it as having two groups of people. Some are undergraduates and some are female. Some are BOTH. The percentage that you use depends on the group of people that you are referring to, and this will depend on your hypothesis.

Layered crosstabs
It is possible to put more than two variables into a table, and this can be useful to investigate the data in more detail. For instance, using our EU example, if you wanted to look at the views about the domestic situation among all respondents who are both female and undergraduates, you could use a layer.

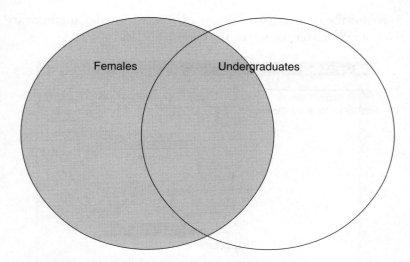

Out of all the females, 44.4 per cent were undergraduates.

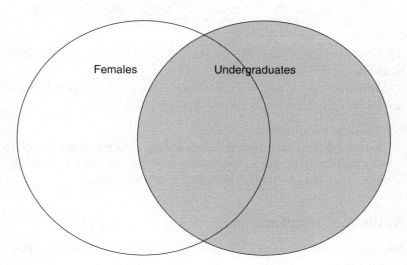

Out of all the undergraduates, 40 per cent were females.

Follow the steps above to create a Crosstab but add another variable into the Layer section of the table (as below).

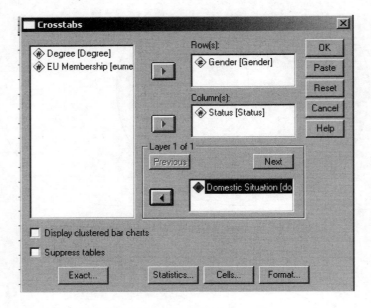

This will bring up a table like the one opposite (only part of the table
is shown for the sake of clarity).

We should add a note of caution here – try not to create tables that
are too complicated for two main reasons:

1. They are very difficult to read!
2. You should be careful not to subdivide the data too often – remember that we have cautioned against this since smaller and smaller
   groups of data will affect the validity of the findings.

Statistical significance

Well, this is all very exciting, but do your results actually MEAN
anything?

Unfortunately, here we have to digress into the world of statistics.
We will try to be brief.

You may have found some very interesting differences between
groups of people and the answers they gave, but in order to make your

Gender * Status * Domestic Situation Crosstabulation

Domestic Situation: Very Good

			Status		
			Undergra-duate	Postgraduate	Total
Gender	Female	Count	2	1	3
		% within Gender	66.7%	33.3%	100.0%
		% within Status	66.7%	100.0%	75.0%
		% of Total	50.0%	25.0%	75.0%
	Male	Count	1	0	1
		% within Gender	100.0%	.0%	100.0%
		% within Status	33.3%	.0%	25.0%
		% of Total	25.0%	.0%	25.0%
Total		Count	3	1	4
		% within Gender	75.0%	25.0%	100.0%
		% within Status	100.0%	100.0%	100.0%
		% of Total	75.0%	25.0%	100.0%

arguments more powerful, you can also run certain tests to see whether these differences are likely to apply to a wider population (assuming you have been careful in selecting your sample) or whether they are simply due to chance.

The social sciences generally use a 95 per cent level of significance – that is, if the probability of getting the results you have is less than 5 in 100 then they can be said to be statistically significant.

Again this goes back to the idea of testing the *Null hypothesis* (see Chapter 2) – the seemingly perverse idea of trying to falsify your results. Think of it as the great detective Sherlock Holmes did: if you eliminate all the other possibilities then what you have is likely to be the truth.

Tests of statistical significance will give you a value that ranges from 0.00 to 1.00, where 1.00 expresses a probability that your results are entirely due to chance, and therefore not something that would apply to a wider population (see Chapter 4). So, what you are hoping for is a low probability – less than 0.05 (less than a 5 per cent likelihood of being due to chance). This is expressed in the following formula:

$$p < 0.05$$

In English, **p** (the probability of the result being due to chance) < (is less than) **0.05** (5%).

It is important to bear in mind that tests of statistical significance make certain assumptions:

1. The tests you can use depend on the type of data that you have. With nominal data, the only test you can legitimately use is *Chi-square* (explained below).
2. All tests assume that you have a representative, random sample (so that they can test whether your findings are likely to apply to the wider population that you have sampled from).
3. 'Significance' is a specific term in this context – it does not necessarily mean 'important'.
4. A test that is not statistically significant is NOT 'insignificant' – it may in fact be one of the most important findings of your research (see Chapter 11). Tests that give probability levels greater than 0.05 can be said to be 'approaching significance' if they are 0.06 or 0.07. Anything greater than 0.05 is expressed as $p > 0.05$.

Chi-square

This test is most often used with Crosstabs. In very simple terms, what the test does is build a table that has the same cells as yours and throws data into it on the basis that there is no relationship between the two things you are testing. It then compares these data (which you might expect to get by chance – there is no relationship) and the data that you have (which you are hoping is not due to chance). If the data you have are different from those which you would expect to get with no relationship between the two, then the test will return a probability less than 0.05.

To add a chi-square test to your Crosstab, follow the steps below:

1. Set the requirements for the Crosstab as outlined above.
2. Click on the *Statistics . . .* button.
3. Click next to the *chi-square* box so that it has a tick in it (see figure opposite).

A statistically significant chi-square will appear below your Crosstab and will look like the table shown opposite.

The figure you are mainly interested in is in the top right corner, under the *Asymp Sig (2-sided)* heading ('Asymptotic Significance' – please don't worry too much about what this term means!). Here, the probability of obtaining these results by chance is 0.000 (expressed to

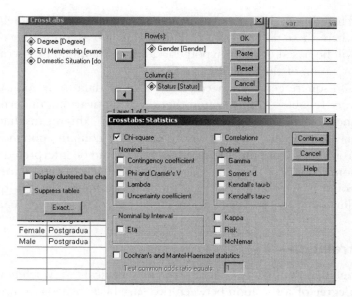

Chi-Square Tests

	Value	df	Asymp. Sig. (2-sided)
Pearson Chi-Square	123.000[a]	3	0.000
Likelihood Ratio	168.680	3	0.000
Linear-by-Linear Association	101.171	1	0.000
N of Valid Cases	123		

a. 0 cells (0.0%) have expected count less than 5. The minimum expected count is 8.34.

three decimal places – there are some numbers in there somewhere, but basically the probability of obtaining this result by chance is very low. It is certainly a lot less than 0.05, so we can say that there are significant differences in this Crosstab.

There are some important aspects to remember about chi-square in addition to those that apply to all statistical tests:

1. The test does not 'know' anything about your data. It simply looks at chance data.

2. Therefore, it does not explain any differences; nor does it tell you where these differences are. This is your job as a researcher and will be based on your hypotheses and your common-sense interpretation of the table itself.
3. Chi-square generally needs quite a lot of data to be robust (i.e. very reliable). You may find that there is a warning underneath the table that concerns the 'expected count' – this means that you have some cells that are empty or do not contain enough data. You can still use the findings, but they should be interpreted with some caution if the percentage of cells with less than the expected count is very high (note that the message below the chi-square illustrated requires each cell to contain a count of more than 5).

Correlation

Correlation is a slightly different type of statistical test which looks at the degree of association between two variables – whether scores on one variable are reflected in scores on another variable. This is most commonly used with data that come from Likert scales (see Chapter 3) and can give some indication of whether answers to questions that aim to measure attitudes, beliefs or consumption habits are related in some way. Using our EU example, we might hypothesise that people who think that the UK domestic situation is good will also approve of joining the EU (for whatever reason).

Again, there are important considerations to bear in mind when using correlations:

1. Data MUST be at least ordinal. This test cannot be used with nominal data. Data that meet this requirement can be tested using the *Spearman* correlation. Data that are of a higher level (interval or ratio) can be tested using the *Pearson* correlation.
2. The test only gives an indication of association – a significant correlation does not mean that scores on one variable CAUSE scores on another variable.
3. Again, a significant correlation does not explain WHY the data might be related. This is your job as a researcher, and you should always bear in mind that there might be a third variable involved – for example, people who think the domestic situation is

good and also approve of EU membership may do so because they are parents and the EU is proposing some specific policy concerning children.

To run a correlation:

1. From the *Analyse* menu –

   Correlate –

   Bivariate . . .

   This will bring up a box like the one shown below.
2. Select one of the variables you want to look at from the list on the left (click on it once so that it is highlighted).
3. Click on the right arrow. This will remove that variable from the first list and place it in the *Variables* list on the right.
4. Follow the same procedure to add the second variable.
5. For ordinal data, check the box next to Spearman, for interval or ratio data, check the box next to Pearson.
6. Click *OK.*

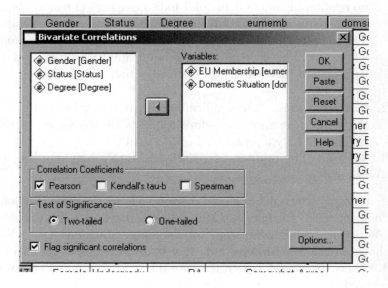

This will produce a correlation in the output window like the one shown overleaf.

Correlations

			EU Membership	Domestic Situation
Spearman's rho	EU Membership	Correlation Coefficient	1.000	0.620**
		Sig. (2-tailed)	.	0.004
		N	20	20
	Domestic Situation	Correlation Coefficient	0.620**	1.000
		Sig. (2-tailed)	0.004	.
		N	20	20

**. Correlation is significant at the 0.01 level (2-tailed).

Correlations (both Pearson and Spearman) compare scores on one variable with scores on another and look for a relationship.

You can see from this table that there are four cells, some of which are redundant (see below), which contain three pieces of information:

1. The *correlation coefficient* – This is the product of complicated calculations that SPSS performs behind the scenes. Coefficients can range from 0 to 1 and basically express the strength of the relationship between the two variables. A figure of 0 indicates that there is no relationship and a figure of 1 indicates a perfect relationship.

   They can also be positive or negative – a positive correlation indicates that both variables are scoring in the same direction, while a negative correlation would indicate that as scores on one variable are increasing, scores on the other are decreasing (and vice versa).

2. The *Sig. (2-tailed)* – the significance level (the probability of getting this result by chance). As before, a statistically significant correlation would have a probability of less than 0.05.

3. The *N* – The number of paired scores (N) that went into the calculation.

Looking at the table you can see some cells are the same. Top left is comparing EU membership with EU membership, bottom right is comparing domestic situation with domestic situation. These both show perfect relationships, indicated by a correlation coefficient of 1.000 (as you would expect, they are the same thing) and so can be ignored.

Top right and bottom left are also the same – they are comparing EU membership with domestic situation – so you only need to look at one of these to see the results of the test.

First, the coefficient is 0.620. This may not seem particularly strong, but it is definitely closer to 1 than it is to 0. There is some debate about what constitutes a 'strong' relationship from correlations (see, for example, Wimmer and Dominick 2006), but very strong relationships are quite rare in the social sciences. Again, this is an area where the researcher must use common sense in interpretation.

Nonetheless, this indicates some sort of positive relationship between the two scores – the correlation coefficient would have a minus sign in front of it if it were negative.

Second, this relationship is statistically significant, as indicated by a significance level of 0.004 in the table. SPSS also usefully indicates this with the ** symbol next to the coefficient. If you look below the table you can see that SPSS tells us that the correlation is significant at the 0.01 level – even less likely to be due to chance than the 0.05 level.

As a final note of caution, correlations do not tell you WHERE the relationship lies, just that there is one. In this case, it could be that a lot of people are responding at the high end of both scales, but it could equally be that they are responding at the low end of both scales. To investigate the nature of the relationship you need to run a separate Crosstab to look at the data in more detail.

Chapter 11 deals with presentation of results in more details.

Presenting Results

This chapter illustrates how to present the findings of your research, how students have used the tests outlined in the previous chapter in their research project, and how they have interpreted and presented their findings.

As examples, we have used various student projects conducted as part of MA programmes at the Cardiff School of Journalism, Media and Cultural Studies. Most of these were part of a ten-week course in quantitative research methods, but projects were conceived, conducted and reported in around five weeks. Details of the requirements and timetable are included in Chapter 12, but essentially the students were asked to design, conduct, analyse and report a project of their own choice. The reporting took the form of a class presentation and a 1,500-word journal article.

Presenting findings

Whether you are presenting your work as a report, journal article or as a visual presentation, there are several elements that are common to good practice.

Introduction

Our students are required to give a selection of academic sources as background to the project – a kind of mini-literature review that sets out the topic area, established thinking and gives an indication of how they came up with their ideas and hypotheses. This will put the research in perspective for the reader/audience and set the scene for outlining the hypotheses and presenting and interpreting the original findings.

Sample and demographics

It's always useful to begin by describing the sample from which your data come. This will put your findings in perspective for the reader/audience.

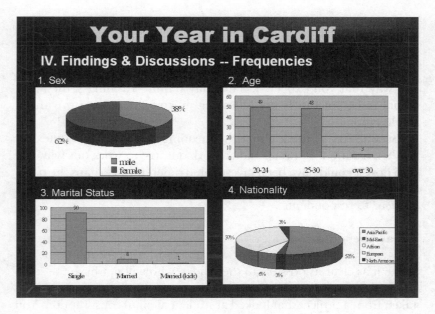

Whether you use tables or graphs is an aesthetic choice, but graphs are often preferred as they convey simple information quickly and easily. (See Appendix 1 for some simple instructions on creating graphs in SPSS.)

Above is a simple PowerPoint slide that uses a variety of graph types to demonstrate the sample from a project.

Key findings

Your key findings are those that directly relate to your hypotheses. Having run a number of statistical tests it's tempting to include all of them, since you went to the trouble of doing them, but it's important that you include only those that are relevant to the research and that relate to the hypotheses that were specified in advance of the analysis.

Not all of these will have worked out the way you hoped, but it is just as important to report these (see below) as it is to report the ones that came out as you predicted and were statistically significant.

'Negative' findings

Analyses that don't work out the way you had anticipated can often be baffling and disappointing. Try to keep an open mind if this happens as these can often be the most interesting and useful parts of your study.

First, assuming that your hypotheses were based on some reasonable thinking, try to work out why they might not have come out the way that you expected. This may require running some additional tests, but this is not 'cheating' if you can come up with an explanation.

Second, try to think about the meaning of this in the context of further research. If things didn't work out, try to work out why, but also how it could have been investigated differently. Perhaps the questions you asked didn't quite get to the heart of the topic or were unclear to respondents.

Clear presentation

However you decide to present your findings, it's important that you make it as clear as possible to the reader, who will not have the same in-depth knowledge of your project as you do. Opposite are two slides taken from a project that looked at student alcohol consumption. You can see that the first presents a fairly complicated **Crosstab** that is difficult to read on paper, let alone on screen. Fortunately, the students did a reasonable job of compressing these data and expressing them slightly differently on the slide that followed, which made things far easier for the audience to see their main finding on this point.

On p. 160 is a good example of how a graph can be used to express quite complicated findings. This is taken from a project that looked at how overseas students (non-UK in this case) and home students (UK in this case) were planning to spend their Christmas vacation. The group suggested that, based on the fact that international students had travelled some distance to come to study, they may be more likely to use vacation time to explore further. They had several breakdowns of these findings and explored them in greater depth, but the graph clearly demonstrates that international students appear more likely to travel during vacations than stick with a single destination.

Statistical significance

Ideally, you should always present the statistical tests that accompany your data, either with an example of the **chi-square** or **correlation**

Findings

Degree * How much? Crosstabulation

				How much?						Total
			Not applicable	1	2	3	4	5	Other	
Degree	Undergradu	Count	0	1	5	10	5	15	10	46
		% within Degree	.0%	2.2%	10.9%	21.7%	10.9%	32.6%	21.7%	100.0%
		% within How m	.0%	16.7%	29.4%	50.0%	50.0%	60.0%	71.4%	48.9%
		% of Total	.0%	1.1%	5.3%	10.6%	5.3%	16.0%	10.6%	48.9%
	Postgraduat	Count	2	5	12	10	5	10	4	48
		% within Degree	4.2%	10.4%	25.0%	20.8%	10.4%	20.8%	8.3%	100.0%
		% within How m	100.0%	83.3%	70.6%	50.0%	50.0%	40.0%	28.6%	51.1%
		% of Total	2.1%	5.3%	12.8%	10.6%	5.3%	10.6%	4.3%	51.1%
Total		Count	2	6	17	20	10	25	14	94
		% within Degree	2.1%	6.4%	18.1%	21.3%	10.6%	26.6%	14.9%	100.0%
		% within How m	100.0%	100.0%	100.0%	100.0%	100.0%	100.0%	100.0%	100.0%
		% of Total	2.1%	6.4%	18.1%	21.3%	10.6%	26.6%	14.9%	100.0%

Analysis

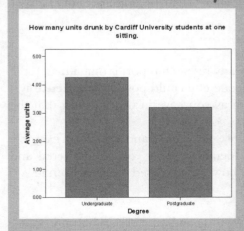

How many units drunk by Cardiff University students at one sitting.

·On average undergraduates drank 1 unit more than postgraduates.

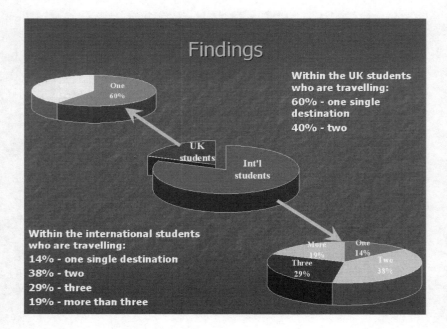

table or by using the notation p < 0.05 or p > 0.05. (See Chapter 10 for more information on running and interpreting these tests.)

Remember that tests that didn't turn out to be statistically significant should be mentioned; your 'negative' findings could be very important.

Replicability

An important requirement of any research report is that it details the methodology. This is so someone else could possibly **replicate** it – that is, run the same research as you have in order to test that the results stand up.

You should give full details of your sample and include an example questionnaire, as well as the details of how you administered and coded the questionnaire, and how you analysed the data from it.

Benefits

Finally, writing up a project like this can have benefits beyond getting a good grade for the research methods course.

A grounding in quantitative research, and practical experience of conducting, analysing, interpreting and presenting it, are important skills to have and it's worth pointing this out to potential employers. Some students have taken copies of work that they have done to job interviews and others have sent 'executive summaries' of research findings to companies that participated as a thank you for their help. This can result in a job offer!

Several former students have contacted us to say that the SPSS skills that they were so wary of at first have come in very useful in their careers at some stage.

CHAPTER 12

Information for Teachers

This chapter sets out some of the pedagogic aspects of teaching quantitative methods in the ways that we have over the last few years. Although we do not claim to teach quantitative methods in great depth, either theoretically or practically, we have found that a simple introduction can be extremely useful to students, especially those with a morbid fear of numbers. Since quantitative methods involve a certain rigour of thought and procedure, we have also found that a short, practical course in questionnaire design and analysis can introduce students to the skills involved in conducting any research project, regardless of the method they choose.

What do students learn?

We focus very much on the practical elements of this course – learning through doing. It is extremely difficult to teach quantitative methods to reluctant students through a series of lectures, especially if you are trying to illustrate the complexities of data analysis. The process of coming up with their own ideas, discovering and (hopefully) solving potential problems, analysing data that they are personally interested in and critiquing each others' work, means that the students learn a great deal (almost without realising it).

Whether the course takes the form of a few practical sessions or a longer core module, we have found the following elements and outcomes are common to introducing students to these sorts of methods. Believe it or not, much of this can be achieved in as little as eight hours of class time. We have included a sample timetable (below, pp. 166–9) to illustrate how this might be done.

Topic choice

Students are encouraged to come up with their own ideas for a short research project. The only restrictions are that they must be able to complete the project in the time allowed, with the resources available.

Generally, they form groups (around four or five in each group seems to work well) and begin by brainstorming for possible topic choices.

Students learn to function as a research team. This is an important skill as 'real-world' research, whether academic or commercial, is increasingly conducted by teams of researchers, often with cross-disciplinary backgrounds and skills. This is a useful experience for any individual student interested in conducting research. They learn that the world's problems cannot be solved by one investigation, and that some methods suit particular topics more than others.

Following on from this, the process of narrowing the research area into a workable project and further defining and redefining their questions to produce hypotheses helps to focus on the topic in hand, to shape their methodology, to define their sample (and population) and to begin to think about ways in which they might phrase their questions and design their questionnaire.

An additional bonus is that they begin to think more critically about published research, as they gain insight into the whole process through personal experience.

Introduction to statistics

Clearly, since this is a quantitative course, students should pick up a basic knowledge of statistics. This is more than the mechanics of SPSS and more than a grasp of the concept of statistical probability. We aim to encourage students to be sceptical about the everyday use and abuse of statistics that we all encounter on television, in newspapers and potentially in their professional careers.

We would hope that when a percentage is casually presented as a compelling fact during a news broadcast, students will automatically begin to ask:

- Exactly WHO was asked this question (the sample)?
- How MANY people were asked this question (the sample size)?
- What EXACTLY were they asked (the question wording and any leading phrases)?

Questionnaire design

A basic familiarity with SPSS (or other statistical programmes), however, will also lead to a better developed questionnaire. Once students have seen what the software can do, and what sort of analyses are common to questionnaire data, they begin to see how a questionnaire can be designed to produce data that will be more capable of answering their research questions and hypotheses.

Practical experience of designing a questionnaire will also reinforce the idea of keeping the hypotheses simple and focused, and also of maintaining strict **operational definitions** of the concepts they are investigating.

Collecting data

The process of collecting data is also a useful experience in the whole research process. It brings home the necessity to be organised, in terms of numbering questionnaires, keeping track of which group members have collected what amount of data, and so on. It can also be fun. It will certainly demonstrate how quantitative methods allow the researcher to gather large amounts of data in a relatively short time.

Analysing data and interpreting findings

This really is an intellectual skill and takes time to get to grips with. However, we believe that the fact that the students have generated their own topics and hypotheses adds motivation and meaning to the analysis side of things. What we are trying to foster here is not simply an understanding of basic statistics and quantitative methods generally, but also a rigorous, sceptical and disciplined approach to their work that is transferable to any form of research, regardless of methodology.

Presenting data

We often assess this sort of project in two ways – by a class presentation (usually using some sort of presentation software such as PowerPoint) and by a written account of the project in the form of a short journal article.

These have common elements in that they necessitate concise presentation and the ability to pick out the key findings of the project. They also require that the students target the presentation to a particular audience – they are encouraged to take the presentations seriously and to present their findings in an academic manner. It would be equally possible to construct an assessment where the target audience is different – for example, to present to a particular commercial audience, or a policy group (a test of their ability to explain quantitative findings to a 'lay' audience – i.e. those not too familiar with the terminology of scientific research).

Giving a class presentation brings further benefits. We tend to use PowerPoint to demonstrate the clarity of thought required to present the entire project in ten minutes – from background literature to future directions – and to present slides that are useful for the audience, without being crammed full of text or overwhelming with rainbow graphics and flashy effects. Of course, this has an additional benefit for the teacher in that students get some experience of being in a teacher's shoes – talking to a room full of people who are not necessarily fascinated by the subject matter. Also they should also begin to appreciate the hours we put into preparation!

A written report of the project can be useful as an example of concise portrayal of the project within a tight word limit, a skill that will often be useful later in their professional careers.

Project critique

A final requirement of the presentation of the project is that the students reflect on the whole experience and on particular elements of their research project.

It's useful to think about what worked and what didn't work; how the questionnaire or the sampling could have been improved; what would be done differently given a second chance, or more time and resources; how the study might be expanded further, or taken in a new direction, as a result of this initial attempt, and so on.

Again this is all part of the learning-through-doing approach, and we have found that often students gain the most from the mistakes that they made, and from the views and input of their classmates.

Assessing the work

In our sessions, we have found that a combination of class exercises and formal work is useful.

Class exercises

One or two simple exercises, completed during class time when the lecturer is present, that aim to ensure that students have grasped the basics of data input, analysis and interpretation.

As previously mentioned, we use our EU 'baby questionnaire' as an example – providing them with data to input that have been carefully constructed to give statistically significant results when analysed.

Project report and presentation

The requirements for these are outlined at the end of this chapter. The benefits have already been mentioned, but the point is to introduce students to public and written presentation skills for a specific audience, and this can be the beginnings of academic writing skills.

Sample timetable

This sets out a timetable for a four-session course with each session lasting two hours. Most of the work (apart from data-gathering) can be achieved within the class time. Although it seems daunting for students and teachers alike, we are constantly amazed at the quality of work produced by students during such a short exposure to quantitative methods.

As we always reiterate, this course is not meant to be a comprehensive explanation of the theory and practicalities of these techniques, but a simple, hands-on approach can give a meaningful and useful introduction to something that many students find difficult and off-putting.

Session 1
Taught content
- Why use quantitative methods?

Because they are compelling and 'scientific'.

Because they appear everywhere in the media, in reports and in published research.

Conducting a quantitative project will give students some understanding of the process of generating numbers and statistics, as well as the process of analysing and presenting them.

• Introduction to SPSS

We use our EU 'baby questionnaire' to illustrate questionnaire design – the demographic and research question components – and also to introduce the ideas of coding real-life data into numbers that can be analysed simply and quickly.

The SPSS environment is explained (as in Chapter 10) and students are talked through setting up one variable and entering some data.

Having completed the first part of the class exercise (see below), the procedures for generating Frequencies, Crosstabs and Correlations are explained and examples are given to illustrate how to read these tables.

Class work
• Introduction to SPSS

They are given a handout with twenty completed EU questionnaires and asked to complete the other four variables in variable view, and then to enter the data from the twenty completed questionnaires.

They are then given some fairly straightforward questions to answer using **Frequencies**, **Crosstabs** and **Correlation**.

This can often be a daunting first taste of quantitative methods, but most students find it satisfying that they can at least enter data into software that many have never used before.

Session 2
Taught content
• Introduction to statistics

Demonstrations of how to run **Frequencies, Crosstabs** (with **chi-square**) and **Correlation**.

This session also includes a section on statistical probability.

Most of this material is covered in Chapter 10.

Class work
- Running the tests

We give a handout with five simple questions about the EU data. Instructions are to type the questions in Word, run the appropriate tests in SPSS and then answer the questions in as much or as little detail as students feel necessary, with supporting tables copied from their SPSS outputs (see p. 189).

Experience of using SPSS on sample data can inform the ways in which students design their own projects and also give them ideas about the sorts of questions that SPSS can help to answer.

Session 3
Taught content
- Research design

Hypotheses and research questions – coming up with a workable idea for a small group project, given the time and resources available.

Sampling – an introduction to the ideas behind sampling so that students are at least aware of the considerations were they to embark on a full-scale research project.

- Questionnaire design

The importance of clear presentation and ethical considerations.

This includes examples of **demographic** and **research question** sections (see Chapter 6), as well as examples of **Likert scales**.

Class work
- Forming groups, topic choice and questionnaire design

Designing a draft questionnaire for piloting.
Thinking about the SPSS coding frame.
Finding relevant background literature.
This can be a useful class debate, and we usually end this part of the session by asking each group to give details of:

- the topic;
- the hypotheses;
- the sample.

• Designing a draft questionnaire

The groups are then required to begin to design their own questionnaire. Ideally, they will print out copies and ask classmates for feedback. This is all part of the **piloting** process and the class should finish with a more or less final version which they can take away to gather data before the final session.

Session 4
Taught content
• Statistics revisited

Much of the session on running the statistical tests is repeated so that students grasp not only the mechanics of SPSS, but also the concept of statistical significance and of how to interpret the more complicated Crosstabs and Correlations.

Class work
• Data analysis and report writing

In this four-session version we tend not to require a class presentation, but assessing the ways in which individual students have understood the process of using SPSS and the results of their own group project can be equally effective.

Group presentation guidelines

This will be a short presentation based on the group work that you have done during this semester.

Each presentation will last no more than TEN MINUTES, followed by time for any questions that the audience may have.

The presentation should ideally be made using PowerPoint, and should contain the following sections:

• Background and rationale – a brief introduction to the topic, explaining why your group decided to investigate it. This should include at least TWO sources of information (books, journal articles, websites, facts and figures, etc.) that are appropriately referenced.

- Hypotheses/research questions – what were you aiming to discover?
- Method – A description of your sample, how you designed your questionnaire, how you administered it, etc.
- Findings – THREE key findings from your analyses (with supporting tables and graphs). Remember, 'negative' findings (ones that you didn't expect) should be included.
- Discussion/conclusions – What these findings have told you about your topic.
- Critique – What worked and what didn't work; how the study could be improved; how you might plan to extend the study further.

CHAPTER 13

Conclusion and Summary

It might be more accurate to say that this brief chapter is a non-conclusion. This is partly because this book does not strictly need to be read in any particular order, although the first part should certainly be read before embarking on the later ones. We expect the book to be used as a work of reference, with student – and teacher – researchers dipping into it for answers to particular questions. We also expect it to be used in conjunction with more specific media research and other textbooks, which give more detailed answers to specific research questions – for example, for students who want to know more about qualitative methods, or for students who are particularly interested in ethnographic methods. We also expect students, once they have chosen their research topic, to do a lot of wider reading around this particular topic. For instance, if you are doing a content analysis on 'bias in the press', or a project on 'children's responses to toy advertising', we would expect you to read other studies on these topics, and these studies, too, may give you ideas for research designs and methods.

In our Bibliography and Reference section, we mention other books on research method and design which you might find useful. The four mentioned first, we consider 'core' texts, because we have used them extensively ourselves in teaching. However, other teachers may find different texts more accessible and useful, and so other standard research method books are listed here too. We have also listed some specific texts that we ourselves have found useful in specialist areas, such as content analysis, and audiences, including child audiences. But there are many other texts on these topics, and a major part of all research, whether in the humanities or in the sciences, is finding your own 'core' and 'specialist' texts that particularly suit you. So we do not propose these texts as a definitive list; they are simply those we have found useful ourselves, and we welcome suggestions for additions.

Our book is thus not the last word on research methods – far from it. It focuses quite tightly on basic research design principles and simple quantitative methodologies, because we believe that these principles and methods, drawn from social science, are a necessary underpinning to learning about, and doing, research generally. We also believe that basic numeracy – being able to understand and manipulate simple quantitative data (frequencies, crosstabs, ordinal, nominal, interval data, percentages, probabilities, and the like) – is an absolute necessity for anybody calling themselves a trained researcher.

'Do – and I understand'

No research method should be rejected without an understanding of it. We believe that it should not be possible for anybody in professional research fields to say that they 'can't do numbers', even if they don't want to use numbers in their own research. Everybody needs to be able to *understand* numbers in the research that they read, if nothing else. They also need to be able to guide students towards the most appropriate research methods for the students' own chosen topics; sometimes the most appropriate methods will be quantitative, using the basic and invaluable research tools, the questionnaire, or, in the case of content analysis, the coding frame. As we've said, we have proposed these practical approaches to research in the media because, thanks to our various enjoyable experiences of teaching research methods with many different kinds of students on many different kinds of course, we believe in the basic primary school pedagogic principle: 'Hear it – and you will forget. See it – and you will remember. *Do* it – and you will understand.'

Hence there is no real end of the story to give here: there will always be more to say and more to do, and further comments and amendments to be made when it comes to designing, and doing, research with human subjects, and research on human communication. Maybe some of it will come from you.

Good luck!

Bibliography and References

Core media research methods texts

Bauer, M. W. and Gaskell, G. (eds.) (2000) *Qualitative Researching with Text, Image and Sound: A Practical Handbook*, London: Sage.

Field, A. (2005) *Discovering Statistics Using SPSS*, London: Sage.

Machin, D. (2002) *Ethnographic Research for Media Studies*, London: Arnold.

Wimmer, R. D. and Dominick, J. R. (2006, 8th edn.) *Mass Media Research: An Introduction*, Belmont, CA: Wadsworth.

Useful media research methods texts

Alasuutari, P. (1998) *An Invitation to Social Research*, London: Sage.

Barwise, P. and Ehrenberg, A. (1996) *Television and its Audience*, London: Sage.

Deacon, D., Pickering, M., Golding, P. and Murdock, G. (1999) *Researching Communications: A Practical Guide to Methods in Media and Cultural Analysis*, London: Arnold.

Flick, U. (1998) *An Introduction to Qualitative Research*, London: Sage.

Fraser, S., Lewis, V., Ding, S., Kellett, M. and Robinson, C. (2003) *Doing Research with Children and Young People*, Milton Keynes: Open University Press.

Hansen, A., Cottle, S., Negrine, R. and Newbold, C. (1998) *Mass Communication Research Methods*, London: Macmillan.

Jensen, K. B. and Jankowski, N. W. (eds.) (1991) *A Handbook of Qualitative Methodologies for Mass Communication Research*, London: Routledge.

Lindlof, T. R. (1995) *Qualitative Communication Research Methods*, Thousand Oaks, CA: Sage.

Salkind, N. J. (2004) *Statistics for People Who (Think They) Hate Statistics*, London: Sage.

Sarantakos, S. (1998, 2nd edn.) *Social Research*, Basingstoke: Macmillan.

Seale, C. (ed.) (1998) *Researching Society and Culture*, London: Sage.

Silverman, D. (2001) *Interpreting Qualitative Data*, London: Sage.

Van Leeuwen, T. and Jewitt, C. (eds.) (2001) *Handbook of Visual Analysis*, London: Sage.

Williams, M. (2000) *Science and Social Science*, London: Routledge.

Content analysis: broadcasting

Davies, M. M. and Corbett, B. (1997) *Children's Television in Britain: An Enquiry for the Broadcasting Standards Commission*, London: Broadcasting Standards Commission.

Gerbner, G., Gross, L., Morgan, M. and Signorielli, N. (1986) 'Living with television: the dynamics of the cultivation process', in J. Bryant and D. Zillman (eds.), *Perspectives on Media Effects*, Hillsdale, NJ: Erlbaum.

Lewis, J., Brookes, R., Mosdell, N. and Threadgold, T. (2006) *Shoot First and Ask Questions Later: Media Coverage of the 2003 Iraq War*, New York: Peter Lang.

Wober, M. and Gunter, B. (1988) *Television and Social Control*, Aldershot: Gower Press.

Research on audiences: some useful readings

Abercrombie, N. and Longhurst, B. (1998) *Audiences: A Sociological Theory of Performance and Imagination*, London: Sage.

Ang, I. (1993) *Desperately Seeking the Audience*, London: Routledge.

Barwise, P. and Ehrenberg, A. (1996) *Television and its Audience*, London: Sage.

Tulloch, J. (2000) *Watching Television Audiences: Cultural Theories and Methods*, London: Arnold.

Media effects and special audiences

Barker, M. and Petley, J. (1997, reprinted 2001) *Ill Effects: The Media Violence Debate*, London: Routledge.

Davies, M. M. (2001) *Dear BBC: Children, Television Storytelling and the Public Sphere*, Cambridge: Cambridge University Press.

Gunter, B. (1992) *Violence and the Mass Media*, London: John Libbey.

Livingstone, S. and Lunt, P. (1994) *Talk on Television: Audience Participation and Public Debate*, London: Routledge.

General references

Aitchison, J. (1983) *The Articulate Mammal*, London: Hutchinson.

Bandura, A., Ross, D. and Ross, R. (1963) 'Imitation of film mediated aggressive models', *Journal of Abnormal and Social Psychology*, vol. 66, No.1, 3–11.

Carter, C. and Davies, M. M. (2004) '"A fresh peach is easier to bruise": children and traumatic news', in S. Allen (ed.), *Journalism: Critical Issues*, Maidenhead and New York: Open University Press, pp. 224–35.

Curran, J. and Seaton, J. (1997) *Power without Responsibility: The Press and Broadcasting in Britain*, London: Routledge.

Davies, M. M., and Mosdell, N. (2001) *Consenting Children?: The Use of Children in Non-fiction Television Programmes*, London: Broadcasting Standards Commission.

Davies, M. M. and Pearson, R. E. (2003) 'Stardom and Distinction: Patrick Stewart as an Agent of Cultural Mobility: A Study of Theatre and Film Audiences in New York City', in M. Barker and T. Austin (eds.), *Contemporary Hollywood Stardom*, London: Arnold, pp. 167–86.

Davies, M. M. and Pearson, R. E. (2004) 'To boldly bestride the narrow world like a colossus: Shakespeare, *Star Trek* and the European TV Market', in I. Bondebjerg and P. Golding (eds.), *European Culture and the Media: Changing Media, Changing Europe*, Vol. 1, Bristol: Intellect Books, pp. 65–90.

Davies, M. M., Lloyd, E. and Scheffler, A. (1987) *Baby Language*, London: Unwin Hyman.

Habermas, J. (1989) *The Transformation of the Public Sphere*, Cambridge: Polity (German original 1962, Luchterhand).

Kuhn, T. (1970) *The Structure of Scientific Revolutions*, Chicago: University of Chicago Press.

Livingstone, S. (2002) *Young People and New Media*, London: Sage.

Livingstone, S. and Bovill, M. (1999) *Children, Young People and the Changing Media Environment*, London: LSE.

Miller, T., Govil, N., McMurria, J., Maxwell, R. and Wang T. (2005) *Global Hollywood 2*, London: British Film Institute.

Pearson, R. E. and Davies, M. M. (2005) 'Class Acts? Public and Private Values and the Cultural Values of Theatre-goers', in S. Livingstone (ed.), *Audiences and Publics: When Cultural Engagement Matters for the Public Sphere*, Bristol: Intellect Books.

Popper, K. (1959) *The Logic of Scientific Discovery*, New York: Basic Books.

Rolston, B. and Miller, D. (1996) *War and Words: The Northern Ireland Media Reader*, Belfast: Beyond the Pale Press.

Wimmer, R. D. and Dominick, J. R. (1994, 4th edn.) *Mass Media Research: An Introduction*, Belmont, CA: Wadsworth.

APPENDICES

1. Graphs

One of the most simple and clear ways to present data is to put them in a graph. This can present your findings in a visually compelling way and spare the reader the task of wading through a series of complicated tables to get at your key findings.

The SPSS[1] program has a wide range of graph templates. It is worth experimenting with these, but beware of blinding your reader with style over content. The purpose of a graph is to display information in a clear and concise way, not to demonstrate that your printer can cope with 256 colours, or that what you really wanted to be was a graphic designer.

In journal articles and reports the two most common graph formats are the **bar graph** and the **pie chart**.

Simple bar graphs

Used to display frequencies. Go to:

1. *Graphs*
2. *Bar . . .*
3. Select *Simple* and click *Define*

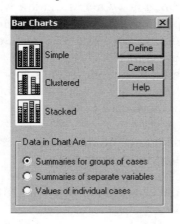

---

[1] This section is based on SPSS version 12.0. Other versions of the software may change some of the cosmetic aspects of graphs, but the basic procedures will be similar.

This will bring up a dialogue box like the one below.

1. Select the variable that you want to display from the list on the left and add it to *Category Axis*: using the arrow key.
2. Change *Bars Represent* to *% of cases* by clicking on the circle.

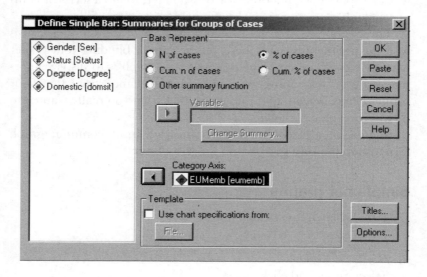

When you click *OK*, a new Output window will open containing your lovely bar graph. If you then double-click anywhere inside the graph, another window will open (SPSS Chart Editor) which allows you to change the appearance of the graph.

Play around with aspects of the graph's appearance. Each time you make a change you can see how it will look by closing the Chart Editor: click *Apply* and then click *Close*.

Changing the appearance of the bars

This will allow you to print in black and white.

Click once on the bars so that they are selected (they have a border around them, as in the Chart Editor box on p. 181).

Click on *Fill & Border*.

Change the colour by selecting a new colour from the palette.

Click *Apply*.

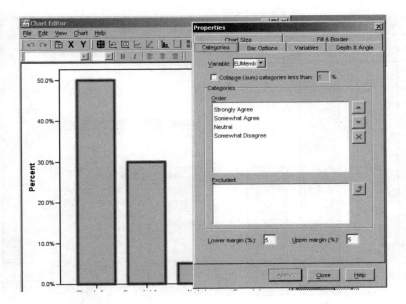

To change the pattern
Click on the bar.
　Click on *Pattern*, and select a pattern from the drop-down menu.
　Change the colour of the bar to white.
　Click *Apply*.

Changing the axis scales
Double click on the axis scale (the labels along the side of the graph
(0, 10, 20, etc.).
　From the *Chart* menu, select *Axis* . . . As above this will allow you
to change the axis title and the placement of that title on the graph
(*Left/Bottom; Right/Top, Centre*). You can also change the scale of the
graph by typing in values for minimum and maximum and major and
minor increments.

Displaying data labels
It can be very useful to display the values that are represented in
graphs.
　In the Chart Editor window, click once on the bars of the graph
(or the slices in a pie chart) so that they are highlighted.

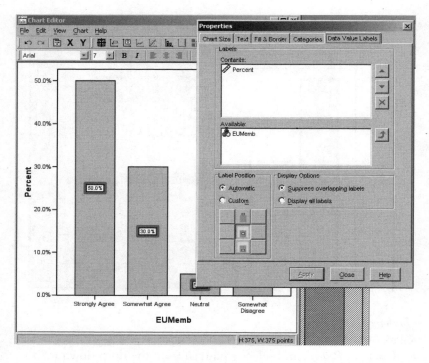

Go to the *Chart* menu and select Show Data Labels.

This will bring up a box like the one above, where the measure you have used (in this case percentage) is automatically inserted.

Play around

Double clicking anything on the graph while inside Chart Editor will bring up options to change that element's properties.

Clustered bar graphs

Bar graphs are very useful to display the results of crosstabs clearly and simply.

Follow the steps above but select *Clustered* from the first screen. This will allow you to plot one variable against another, for example, Gender against EU membership.

You will initially get a hideous rainbow of colours, but you can change the colour and fill style of each bar in the variable by following the steps above.

Pie charts

It's easiest to use these for simple frequencies.

Go to the *Graphs* menu and select *Pie* . . . then follow the steps outlined above for a simple bar graph.

This will give you a Pie Chart which you can edit as above, but with the added excitement of being able to emphasise the importance of slices by taking them out of the pie – click on a slice, go to the *Chart* menu and select *Explode Slice*.

Chart templates

If you are planning to use several graphs, you can save time by creating a chart template so that they all look similar – for example, so that they are all in black and white with patterned fills.

Once you have spent hours editing the appearance of your first graph, open the SPSS Chart Editor, go to the *File* menu and select *Save Chart Template*. This will prompt you for a filename (e.g. Graph-Style1) which you should save somewhere on your hard drive.

When you next go to create a graph, go to the *Graphs* menu and select the style of graph that you want to use.

Define the graph (the variable you want to use and the percentages or counts), but before clicking *OK*, check the box next to *Use chart specifications from*: and click the *File* . . . button.

This will bring up a dialogue box like the one below.

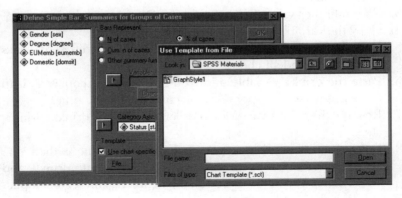

Select your graph template and click *Open*. This should make the graph appear in the style that you have so carefully edited. Or at least something vaguely like it . . .

2. Multiple Responses

Most of our students have had occasions where respondents ticked more than one answer on their questionnaire. There are a few ways of getting around this but a fairly simple one is to create new variables and then add them together in a *Multiple Response Set* to allow you to see how many times a particular response was chosen.

For example, a study investigating British culture may well feature the following question:

Which is your favourite choice of drink when you are in the pub?
Lager   Bitter   Stout   Wine   Absinthe   Gin   Vodka   Fruit-based
beverage

Although you have asked for the respondents' favourite, they may well choose more than one.

You cannot make any decisions about their favourite drink; you have to use the data that are given to you (and refine the question for later use). For the moment, you can make a multiple-response set to determine which drink was chosen most often.

1. Create a new variable in *Variable View* called drink1.
2. Enter the values from 1–8 that correspond to the drinks above (e.g. 1 = lager).
3. Enter another value, 0, that stands for 'Not Applicable'.
4. Copy the variable.
5. Look at your data and find the highest number of different drinks that any respondent chose.
6. Paste the drink1 variable until you have enough copies of it to allow this person's responses to be entered one at a time.
7. Rename the drink1 variables in order (e.g. drink1, drink2, drink3, etc.).
8. Enter your data: Where people have chosen more than one answer, put the first one into drink1, the second into drink2, and so on. When you have entered all their choices, enter 'Not Applicable' for all the other drink variables.

Once you have all the data, you can create the multiple-response set which will allow you to add everything together.

1. From the *Analyse* menu, select *Multiple Response* and *Define Sets . . .*
2. Highlight the variables that you want to include (in this case, all the *drink* variables) and add them to the *Variables in Set:* box using the arrow button.
3. Define the range of values in this variable – From 1 to 8 in this case (do not include 0).
4. Give the set a name and a label (the same as you would when creating a new variable).
5. Click on the *Add* button to place this new set under the *Mult Response Sets:* list on the right-hand side of the screen.
6. Click on *Close*.

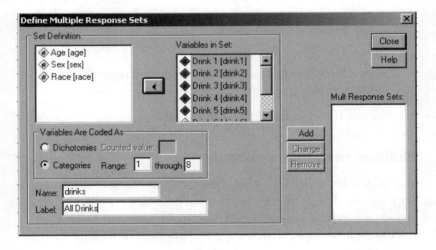

Multiple-response frequencies

You will now notice that there are other options available to you if you go to the *Analyse* menu and select *Multiple Response.*

When you select these new tests they do not appear in quite the same way as before. Overleaf is an example of the Frequency table for this data set:

Category Label – Fairly obvious.

Code – The value that was assigned to it within the drink variable.

Group $ Drink All Drinks

Category label	Code	Count	Pct of Responses	Pct of Cases
Lager	1	5	20.0	33.3
Bitter	2	1	4.0	6.7
Stout	3	4	16.0	26.7
Wine	4	3	12.0	20.0
Absinthe	5	4	16.0	26.7
Gin	6	1	4.0	6.7
Vodka	7	3	12.0	20.0
Fruit-based beverage	8	4	16.0	26.7
Total responses		25	100.0	166.7

0 missing cases; 15 valid cases

Count – How many times that value appeared regardless of which drink variable it was in.

For your analyses use the *Pct of Responses* figure.

Multiple-response crosstabs

You may want to look at some crosstabs that include this multiple response set. This is an ugly process but possible.

Go to the *Analyse* menu, select *Multiple Response* and *Crosstabs* . . .

Add your multiple response set and another variable to the rows and columns as you would do normally.

You will notice that when you add another variable you will have to define the range of that variable. Click on the *Define Ranges* . . . button and enter the minimum and maximum values of that variable.

1. Click on the *Options* button.
2. Check the boxes that will display percentages.
3. Click on the button to change the percentages so that they are based on *Responses*.

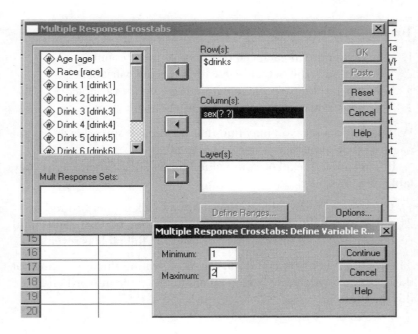

4. Click *Continue*.
5. Click *OK*.

This should present you with a very low-quality table that looks something like a crosstab.

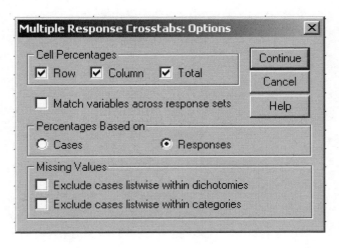

To read the table:

1. The first figure in each cell of the table is the count.
2. The second is the percentage within the row variable.
3. The third is the percentage within the column variable.
4. The final figure is the percentage of the total.

With large data sets you may find that the table is spread over several pages or that some of it is not visible at all.

If you cannot see all of your values displayed in either a frequency table or a crosstab:

1. Click once on the table so that it has a black border around it.
2. Click and hold down on the square in the bottom right-hand corner and drag this downwards until the full table is revealed.

There's not much you can do in terms of editing the appearance of these tables, so probably best to create a new table in word and type this data into it.

3. Example SPSS Exercise

Using the data you have (see data in spreadsheets, pp. 55–6), use the appropriate statistical procedures and tests to find answers to the following questions:

1. Were there equal numbers of subjects (people) from each of the four degrees in the school?

   FREQUENCIES

2. What percentage of all subjects (people) think the overall domestic situation in the UK is very bad?
   What percentage think it is neither bad nor good?

   FREQUENCIES

3. How many women and how many men strongly support Britain's membership of the EU? Express these as a proportion (percentage).

   CROSSTABS

4. What was the distribution of men and women across the four degree programmes? Is this distribution significantly unequal?

   CROSSTABS/statistics = chi-square.

5. Is there any evidence that people who think the situation in the UK is good are also more likely to approve of membership of the EU?

   CORRELATION + CROSSTAB

6. Think of one more question of your own to 'interrogate' these data, and run the appropriate statistical procedure on it.

4. Questionnaire Design Guide

Presentation

If the questionnaire looks professional, so do you. Make sure you spell check! Spend some time on the layout so that the questionnaire looks clear.

Don't make it too long.

Think carefully about the questions that will give you the most useful data. It needs to be completed in a few minutes (especially important if you are stopping people in the street) – 20–30 questions at the most.

The majority of questions should be multiple-choice so that respondents can answer them quickly.

Make sure that your instructions are clear – state whether you want respondents to circle or tick answers and whether they can choose more than one option in particular questions.

Be polite. It's useful to have some sort of introduction at the beginning which explains who you are and what you are doing. Try not to give too much away though. You should usually guarantee that all responses are anonymous and will be used only for academic research.

Always remember to thank respondents for their time at the end. You may also want to include a space at the end for 'any other comments'.

Sections

1. Demographics

This usually comes first as it is a non-threatening way of introducing people to your questionnaire. Think about personal characteristics that will influence the way in which people answer the questions related to your research. For example, will a person's nationality (or country of origin) affect their responses?

Other things to consider might include: age; gender; nationality/ ethnicity; religion; education; income; number of children (and their ages), etc.

Potentially sensitive questions are often phrased so that they are not too specific, for example, using a range of ages or incomes (e.g. 18–21; 22–25, etc).

Think carefully about how you will ask for people's nationality – you are not likely to get equal numbers of respondents from Wales and from Mongolia.

2. 'Lifestyle'

Cultural consumption, taste and attitudes may be relevant to you. You can use multiple-choice or Likert scale questions to investigate this – for example, where people get their news, which newspaper they read, how much television they watch, etc. Do people who read broadsheets think differently about the issue in which you are interested from people who read tabloids?

You may also be interested in how often they purchase a particular product or type of product, where they purchase it and how much they spend.

You may be interested in how often they visit a particular facility (cinema, shopping centre, the Graduate Centre), etc.

3. Research questions

This is the most important part of your questionnaire. It is standard to use Likert scale questions here, where the respondent is asked to give their level of agreement to certain statements, for example:

SPSS is pointless
Strongly Agree   Agree   Neutral   Disagree   Strongly Disagree

Make your statements clear and try to elicit answers that will cover the full range of the scale (be careful not to offend people though). Make sure your respondents will have enough knowledge to answer the question and that the answers are not too obvious. You may also want to consider grouping questions that have the same answer format, but be wary of setting it out in a way that generates automatic responses.

It may be possible to put in some 'decoy' questions to avoid giving away your research hypothesis.

4. Open-ended questions

You may want to include one or two (not more) questions where respondents can answer in more detail. The answers can be post-coded later. This allows you to collect some qualitative data or to gather answers to questions that are difficult to predict. If you use these, put them near the end of the questionnaire – people may be pushed for time and not want to have to think too much.

Other points

Think carefully about how you will code the questionnaire as you construct it. You may want to put your variables into SPSS as you go along.

Too many 'Neutral/Don't Know/Undecided' answers are not desirable. Make the questions bold and thought-provoking. You may also want to include a response of 'Do not wish to answer' for potentially sensitive questions.

If you are concerned about respondents answering randomly, you may want to have a couple of questions that are aimed at the same topic but are worded differently, perhaps even with the scales reversed. This will also avoid 'response set' – automatically answering 'agree' to every question.

Make sure your questions are clear and are addressing exactly what you want them to. Avoid double-questions, for example:

How much do you want to be rich and famous?

Personally, I wouldn't mind being rich but I'm not sure I really want to have to dodge paparazzi every morning.

Avoid hypothetical questions, for example:

When you become rich, what will you spend your money on?

Make sure your respondents have the knowledge to answer the questions, and try to avoid technical jargon. For example:

When you buy your speedboat, will it be the RS105 or the T47 Raptor?

ALWAYS pilot your questionnaire – test it out on other people in the class or on your housemates. This will ensure that your instructions and wording are clear.

Good luck!

Index